CAMBRIDGE LIBRARY COLLECTION

Books of enduring scholarly value

Cambridge

The city of Cambridge received its royal charter in 1201, having already been home to Britons, Romans and Anglo-Saxons for many centuries. Cambridge University was founded soon afterwards and celebrates its octocentenary in 2009. This series explores the history and influence of Cambridge as a centre of science, learning, and discovery, its contributions to national and global politics and culture, and its inevitable controversies and scandals.

Bibliotheca Pepysiana

Samuel Pepys (1633-1703) was a student of Magdalene College, Cambridge, and bequeathed his personal library of 3000 volumes to the College on condition that the contents remained intact and unaltered; they remain there, in his original bookcases, to this day. This descriptive catalogue was published in four volumes, each with a different editor, between 1914 and 1940. Volume 1 lists the 114 manuscripts in Pepys's collection – some dating back to the middle ages – relating to maritime and naval matters, a subject of particular interest to Pepys, who was employed by the admiralty. They fall into three main categories: official documents of his own time, other official and unofficial documents that he collected as material for his projected 'History of the Navy', and books and papers that appealed to him but are not directly relevant to naval history. This volume remains a valuable resource for researchers in naval history.

Cambridge University Press has long been a pioneer in the reissuing of out-of-print titles from its own backlist, producing digital reprints of books that are still sought after by scholars and students but could not be reprinted economically using traditional technology. The Cambridge Library Collection extends this activity to a wider range of books which are still of importance to researchers and professionals, either for the source material they contain, or as landmarks in the history of their academic discipline.

Drawing from the world-renowned collections in the Cambridge University Library, and guided by the advice of experts in each subject area, Cambridge University Press is using state-of-the-art scanning machines in its own Printing House to capture the content of each book selected for inclusion. The files are processed to give a consistently clear, crisp image, and the books finished to the high quality standard for which the Press is recognised around the world. The latest print-on-demand technology ensures that the books will remain available indefinitely, and that orders for single or multiple copies can quickly be supplied.

The Cambridge Library Collection will bring back to life books of enduring scholarly value across a wide range of disciplines in the humanities and social sciences and in science and technology.

Bibliotheca Pepysiana

A Descriptive Catalogue of the Library of
Samuel Pepys

VOLUME 1
PART 1: 'SEA' MANUSCRIPTS

JOSEPH ROBSON TANNER

CAMBRIDGE
UNIVERSITY PRESS

CAMBRIDGE UNIVERSITY PRESS

Cambridge New York Melbourne Madrid Cape Town Singapore São Paolo Delhi

Published in the United States of America by Cambridge University Press, New York

www.cambridge.org
Information on this title: www.cambridge.org/9781108002028

This edition first published 1914
This digitally printed version 2009

ISBN 978-1-108-00202-8

BIBLIOTHECA PEPYSIANA.

PART I.—"SEA" MANUSCRIPTS.

NOTE

Not more than 500 copies of the complete Catalogue will be issued ; but owing to the special appeal made by this and one or two of the subsequent Parts, a limited number of extra copies of such Parts will be printed for independent sale.

The Illustrations, consisting of photographic fac-similes, will be issued in a portfolio as a separate Part.

Part II will contain Mr. E. Gordon Duff's catalogue of *The Early Printed Books*, and the general Introduction.

BIBLIOTHECA PEPYSIANA

A DESCRIPTIVE CATALOGUE OF THE LIBRARY OF SAMUEL PEPYS

PART I. — "SEA" MANUSCRIPTS

By Dr. J. R. TANNER.

—

LONDON:

SIDGWICK & JACKSON, LTD.

MCMXIV

"SEA" MSS.

INTRODUCTION

THAT part of his Collection which Samuel Pepys classified as "Sea" MSS. consists of one hundred and fourteen volumes, the contents of which cover a wide field of naval history. The leading motive of the collector is probably to be found in his projected "History of the Navy." Early in his career he thought of writing a History of the Dutch War, "it being a thing I much desire, and sorts mightily with my genius."[1] Later on the design expanded into a complete naval history,[2] and at the time of his death he was supposed to have been engaged on it for many years.[3] His correspondence with Evelyn and Sir William Dugdale[4] suggests that it would have included in its scope the antiquities of the Navy and possibly the history of navigation, as well as administrative history; and this view is supported by his selection of "Sea" MSS. for his Library. The manuscripts may be roughly classified in three groups :— (i) Official documents of Pepys's own time, the presence of which in the Library may be explained by the predatory

(1) *Diary*, 13 June, 1664.
(2) *Diary*, 16 Jan., 1667-8 ; 15 and 17 Mar., 1668-9.
(3) " This day died Mr. Samuel Pepys, a very worthy, industrious, and curious person, none in England exceeding him in knowledge of the navy. . . . . He had for divers years under his hand the History of the Navy, or *Navalia* as he called it ; but how far advanced, and what will follow of his, is left, I suppose, to his sister's son . . . ." (Evelyn's *Diary*, 26 May, 1703.)
(4) Wheatley, *Pepysiana*, pp. 185-7.

A

habits of retiring officials in his day; (ii) other official and unofficial documents—many of them acquired or copied at some expense—brought together deliberately in order to serve as material for the projected "History of the Navy"; (iii) books and papers which specially appealed to Pepys's characteristic curiosity, and have only an indirect bearing upon naval history.   The line between the last two classes cannot be sharply drawn, as few of the "Sea MSS." are merely curious, and irrelevant to the history of the navy as Pepys himself interpreted it.

(i.)   For the first thirteen years after the Restoration, when Pepys was only Clerk of the Acts, the official documents collected by him refer chiefly to proceedings in which he himself played an important part; but after 1673, when the Clerk of the Acts became Secretary to the Admiralty, and had better opportunities of appropriation, they supply materials for the whole administration of the Navy as far as the Revolution of 1688. The more important of these documents have been described and discussed in the General Introduction to *A Descriptive Catalogue of the Naval Manuscripts in the Pepysian Library at Magdalene College, Cambridge,* now in course of publication by the Navy Records Society. They include : (1) a collection of the original returns on naval matters called for by Parliament from 1660 to the end of Pepys's first Secretaryship in 1679 [Nos. 2265-6] ; (2) materials for estimating the cost of the Second Dutch War [Nos. 2583 and 2589]; (3) materials for the history of the important episode of the Duke of York's remonstrance to the Navy Board in 1668, supplying a reasoned criticism of the higher administration of the Navy during the period of the War [No. 2242] ; (4) Pepys's "Report touching the ancient and present Œconomy of the Navy . . . 17 April, 1669" [No. 2735], and the elaborate and methodical defence of the Navy presented by him to the Commissioners of Public Accounts, 29 November, 1669 [No. 2554]; (5) the materials for a full account of the proceedings of the Special Commission of 1686 [Nos. 1490, 1534, 2823, and 2824], afterwards used by him for his printed *Memoirs of the Royal Navy* ; (6) the establishment for the Office of the Ordnance as confirmed in 1683 and amended in 1687 [No. 2827] ; and (7) registers of ships, guns, officers, and men [Nos. 1340, 2122, 2762, 2940, and 2941], which supply authoritative information upon some points of naval biography and naval equipment.[1] This group of documents also contains collections of considerable importance for the administrative history of the Navy from the Restoration to the Revolution : (8) *Naval and Admiralty Precedents* [No. 2867], "a collection of naval forms and other papers, serving for information and precedents in most of the principal occasions of the Admiralty and Navy calling for the same," from 1660 to 1688[2] ; (9) *Admiralty Letters* [Nos. 2849–62], fourteen volumes containing the correspondence which passed out of Pepys's office during his two Secretaryships, 1673–79 and 1684–88 ; and (10) the *Admiralty Journal* [No. 2865], being the minute-book of the Commission of the Admiralty from 1 January, 1673–4 to 21 April, 1679. Of a somewhat different type, but of no less value to the historian of the Navy, are (11) the entries in *Naval Minutes* [No. 2866], a volume in which Pepys made miscellaneous memoranda, many of them notes for his projected History ; and (12) the *Navy White Book* [No. 2581], in which he noted abuses in shorthand, and wrote down "matters for future reflection" arising out of the Second Dutch War. (13) *King James II's Pocket Book of Rates and Memorandums* [No. 488] is an interesting relic piously preserved, and on the question of wages it has been quoted as an authority.[3]

(ii.) The most substantial works in the category of documents deliberately collected to serve as material for the projected History are : (1) the naval discourses of Sir William Monson [No. 2834], John Hollond [Nos. 2193 and 2835], and Sir Robert Slyngesbie [Nos. 2193 and 2871] ; (2) copious extracts from naval authorities and historians [Nos. 1266, 2197, 2217, 2363, 2643, 2714] carefully indexed either in the volumes

(1) See also Sir Anthony Deane's Report on the French Navy [No. 2241].

(2) *S.P.'s Day Collection* [No. 2902] contains a selection of important papers in constant use by Pepys during his second Secretaryship, 1684–88, but most of them are transcripts of documents to be found elsewhere among "Sea MSS."

(3) *Catalogue of Pepysian MSS.* (*N.R.S.* Publications, vol. xxvi), i. 141.

themselves or separately [Nos. 2846 and 2829]; and (3) Mountgomery's *Book of the Navy* [No. 1774]. The last-named is of special interest because there is reason for thinking that it may have affected English naval policy at a critical point. The treatise was written by Mountgomery for his own amusement; but he showed it to the "principal masters of the Navy," and was by them advised to submit it to "a Parliament Lord," and copies were eventually made for Lords Clinton and Saye and for Leicester himself.[1]   Leicester appears to have taken up Mountgomery's scheme for the distribution of the Royal Navy for home defence in three squadrons on the English coasts and to have urged it in the Council; and it may be that some of the difficulty which Drake had in 1587 and Howard in 1588 in getting leave from the Queen to seek the Spaniards in their own waters may have been due to this cause.   Leicester's copy is in the British Museum.[2]   The same group includes: (4) copies of the official reports of the Commissions of 1608 [No. 2165] and 1618 [No. 2735]; (5) *Edward Fenton's Book*, 1590 [No. 513]; (6) *Miscellaneous Naval Manuscripts* [No. 2911] of the time of James I; (7) Francis Thynne's "collection of matters touching the Constables of Dover Castle and the Wardens of the Five Ports" [No. 1811]; (8) Sir Anthony Deane's "collections" relating to the Navy of France, 1675 [No. 2241]; (9) Penn's *Naval Collections* [No. 2611], being "a collection of several manuscripts taken out of Sir William Penn's closet relating to the affairs of the Navy"; and (10) a copy of Ryther's edition of Petruccio Ubaldino's Discourse on the Spanish Armada [No. 2806].   There are also (11) various volumes relating to shipbuilding [Nos. 1074, 1338, 1339, 1731, 2501, 2820, 2910, 2934] and navigation [Nos. 1825, 2184, 2185], including *A Catalogue to Mr. Pepys's books on Navigation* [No. 2700].   Of these the most important are a curious and valuable work entitled *Fragments of Ancient*

(1) B.M., Add. MSS. 20042.

(2) Add. MSS. 18035.   Other copies are Add. MSS. 20042 and Arundel 22; there is also a 19th century copy of 20042 in Add. MSS. 20043.   All these, except Add. MSS. 18035, contain the addition of 1588 as well as the original treatise of 1570.

English Shipwrightry [No. 2820], and Sir Anthony Deane's *Doctrine of Naval Architecture* [No. 2910], a book described by Evelyn as "an extraordinary jewel." There is also a set of sea-charts [No. 2970], and a Survey of the Thames in 1684 and 1687 [No. 2997], with maps signed by the Principal Officers of the Navy and the Elder Brethren of the Trinity House.

In addition to these separate works there is (12) the large and important collection in eleven volumes, entitled by Pepys *A Miscellany of Matters Historical, Political, and Naval* [Nos. 2869–79]. This contains copies of 1438 documents, transcribed from various sources, and ranging from a complete copy, in 114 folio pages, of Sir Philip Meadows's work on the Sovereignty of the Seas [ix. 2–115] down to "A true Copy of the Great Turke his Stile which he most commonly writeth in His great Affaires" [iii. 56]. It is proposed to catalogue these papers in full in the more elaborate account of the Pepysian Naval MSS. now in course of publication by the Navy Records Society, but considerations of space make this impossible in the present instance. The principle of selection adopted in the text has been to include all papers bearing on the administrative history of the Navy as a modern historian would conceive it, and such other papers as may for any reason be regarded as of special interest[1] or importance. This involves the omission of the greater part of "matters historical and political" and the inclusion of the greater part of "matters naval"; but the omissions are perhaps justified by the fact that a separate volume in the Library [No. 2880] contains the tables of contents of all the volumes of *Miscellanies* re-copied for convenience of reference. The matters included comprise a better copy of Phineas Pett's Journal than the one commonly known [i. 51]; a transcript of the Commonplace Book of Mr. Bedford, the Register of the Admiralty, containing a large number of papers and precedents relating to Admiralty affairs [vol. iv.]; the defence of the Navy Board in connexion with the

(1) The editor has, with some hesitation, included two papers relating to the Tobermory galleon [*Miscellanies*, iv. 510, 511].

failures of the Second Dutch War [vi. 361, 385, 509] ; Sir Anthony Deane's observations on the state of the fleet in 1674 [v. 49] ; the papers presented to Parliament by Pepys in 1675, with his general report on the state of the Navy at that date [v. 185] ; "Mr. Pepys's heads for discourse in Parliament upon the business of the Navy, anno 1676 " [ii. 453] ; a large number of documents relating to naval abuses at various times [iii. 355, 503 ; vii. 145, 158, 183, 270, 273, 361, 382, 388 ; viii. 632 ; x. *passim*] ; papers relating to salutes and the history of the flag [iv. 237 ; v. 235 ; ix. *passim*][1] ; and "The Journal of the Green Ribband Club at the King's Head Tavern over against the Temple in Fleet Street from 1678 to 1681 " [vii. 465], copied from the original lent to Pepys by the king. There are also to be found in these volumes a number of patents, commissions, and lists of ships, as well as papers relating to shipbuilding, victualling, and finance ; also transcripts from the " Black Book of the Admiralty " [iii. 158, 177, 206, 228, 233 ; iv. 515, 759], and collections of papers referring to the Shipwrights' Company [vi. 243–57 ; vii. 421–63] and to the Corporation of Trinity House [i. 1, 22 ; xi. 281, 562–912].

(iii.) The group of books and papers which appealed mainly to the insatiable curiosity of Pepys is not very large. (1) A considerable number of transcripts in the *Miscellanies* are the result of this instinct, and have no bearing upon the history of the Navy. Of this kind are papers relating to Sir William Petty's calculations and experiments [ii. 477, 489 ; v. 559 ; vi. 1, 31, 35], and a copy of " A Discourse made by Sir Robert Southwell before the Royal Society, 8 April, 1675, touching Water " [ii. 505]. These suggest that Pepys's scientific interests were entirely genuine, and were not due, as has been suggested, to a desire to commend himself to the king. On the other hand, it is not easy to see why he should have transcribed for his Collection an index to a volume of papers in the Library of the Dutch Church in London [xi. 161] or an account of the proceedings in the famous case of Godden *v*. Hales in support of James II's claim to

---

(1) *See also* Lieutenant Graydon's *Collection of Naval Flags and Colours*, 1686 [No. 1608].

the dispensing power [xi. 249]. (2) Other volumes, although they relate to naval subjects, are chiefly interesting to the collector, as, for instance, the *Libro de Cargos* [No. 2269], a relic of the Spanish Armada ; a copy of the "Libel of English Policy" [No. 1461]; *An Ancient Discourse and Description of Milford Haven* [No. 1296], "once the Lord Burghley's book"; and "A Project of a form by an Order of Intrenchment for defence against a landing of any army" [No. 2021], also "directed" to Lord Burghley. Perhaps the famous illuminated rolls containing Anthony Anthony's *Declaration of the Royal Navy of England* [No. 2991] should now be included in this category, although no doubt Pepys himself took a much higher view of their value as an historical authority.[1] (3) The collection of voyages and journals among "Sea" MSS.[2] [Nos. 1663, 2133, 2349, 2350, and 2543, 2542, 2584, 2610, 2698, 2813, 2826, 2894] includes the Journals of Sir John Narbrough, 1672–3 [Nos. 2555 and 2556], and *A Collection of Sea Journals* made by Richard Gibson in 1684 [No. 2351]. There is also (4) a copy of Balfour's *Practiques* [No. 2208], the earliest text-book of Scottish law; (5) a volume of papers which are of special importance for the early history of America, entitled *Instructions to Commissioners, and Journals relating to Virginia*, 1676–7 [No. 2582]; and (6) a late addition to the Collection in the form of a criticism of Admiral Russell's Expedition to the Mediterranean of June, 1694 [No. 2276]. (7) A group of presentation works is also of some interest: Henry Shere's *Discourse touching the Current in the Strait of Gibraltar* [No. 1476]; Bolland's *Mediterranean Journal* [No. 2899]; "Mr. Hosier's method of balancing Storekeepers' Accounts" [No. 1788]; a translation of instructions for the Dutch Courts of Admiralty [No. 2060][3]; and Edward Battine's *Method of Building . . . . Ships of War* [No. 977]. The last-named was severely criticised by Pepys for its inaccuracies in a letter

(1) No. 2219 is an illuminated abstract of the Rolls, probably made for Pepys before he acquired the originals.

(2) Voyages and geographical papers are also to be found in the *Miscellanies* [v. 291, 351, 415, 487, 503, 603 ; vi. 271, 333].

(3) *See also* No. 2061.

of 5 January, 1685–6, the substance of which is printed in vol. xxvi of the Navy Records Society's Publications (p. 231).

A more systematic enquiry into the origins of the "Sea" MSS. will be attempted hereafter in connexion with the larger Catalogue of the Navy Records Society, but certain identifications have been already made, and are noted below in the text. In the case of many of the transcripts contained in the *Miscellanies* the sources are indicated by Pepys himself. For instance, some of the papers in vol. i and the whole of vol. viii are from Sir Robert Cotton's Library, and most of those in vol. ii are transcribed from Sir Julius Cæsar's Library; and it has been possible to identify some of them among the Lansdowne and Cottonian MSS. A certain number of the papers in the Pepysian Collection are also to be found in duplicate among the Pepys Papers in the Rawlinson Collection at the Bodleian,[1] more particularly : (1) two versions of the *Register of the Ships of the Royal Navy* [No. 2940], one from 1660 to 1675 [Rawlinson MSS. A. 197. f. 1], and the other extending down to 1686 [*ib.* f. 33], and a register of officers [*ib.* A. 199] very similar to the register in the Pepysian Library [No. 2941]; and (2) a collection of papers [Rawlinson MSS. A. 464] bearing on the establishment of the Special Commission of 1686, and including two copies [ff. 76 and 102] of Pepys's "Memorial and Proposition touching the Navy," dated 26 January and presented to the King 29 January, 1685–6,[2] with a copy of the "Proposition" and the report thereon, dated 30 March, 1686, signed by six of the Officers of the Navy [f. 92].[3] (3) The Rawlinson Collection also contains many volumes of Pepys's miscellaneous correspondence, part of which bears upon the history of the Navy during the period of his administration, and throws light upon the problems raised by the "Sea" MSS. at Magdalene.

Although Pepys retained so many of the official documents relating to the period of his administration, duplicates of two of the most important

---

(1) See also an article by Professor C. H. Firth in the *Mariner's Mirror* for August, 1913, entitled "Papers relating to the Navy in the Bodleian Library."

(2) *cf.* Pepysian MS. No. 1490.   (3) See *Catalogue of Pepysian MSS.*, i. 72.

sets of his papers are in the Admiralty Library in Whitehall. (1) The
Pepysian *Admiralty Letters* [Nos. 2849–2862] are from 19 June, 1673,
to 21 May, 1679, and from 23 May, 1684, to 5 March, 1688–9. The
Admiralty Library contains a series of similar letter-books entitled
Admiralty Letters and Orders [MSS. 14–18] from 2 January, 1673–4,
to 19 May, 1684, and another series entitled *Secretary of Admiralty's
Letters* [MSS. 35–37] from 5 June, 1679, to 30 May, 1684. The former
series also contains orders and warrants for the whole period, which in
the Pepysian series are only entered down to 31 December, 1673; and
there is in the Admiralty Library another series entitled *Orders and
Warrants* [MSS. 9–12, 48] from 18 June, 1673, to 25 December, 1683. It
would therefore appear that, except for the first six months of Pepys's first
Secretaryship, the Admiralty documents are much more complete as far as
1684, and include the period 1679–84, during which Pepys was out of
office, but that from 1684 to 1688 the Pepysian letter-books are probably
unique. (2) Much the same state of things exists with regard to the
minutes of the Admiralty Commission. The Pepysian *Admiralty Journal*
[No. 2865] is from 1 January, 1673–4, to 21 April, 1679. The corresponding
Admiralty Journal in the Admiralty Library [MSS. 41–44] is from 28 June,
1673, to 10 May, 1684[1]; but in this case the minutes for Pepys's second
Secretaryship, from 1684 to 1688, appear to be missing from both Libraries.
Other official papers in the Admiralty Library which should be compared with
the corresponding documents in the Pepysian Library are the following :—
(3) a Register of Officers, 1660–85 [MS. 71], which should be compared
with the Pepysian Register [No. 2941][2]; (4) A record of various commis-

(1) In the Rawlinson MSS. [A. 193. f. 164] are the shorthand minutes of the proceedings of the Admiralty Commission for November and December, 1673, with a note:
"To be entered in longhand in the public minute book thereof"; but in the
Admiralty copy there are no entries between 14 November, 1673, and 1 January,
1673–4.

(2) The Admiralty Library also contains a list of "officers recommended for employment," 1673–89 [MS. 73] classified under offices (captains, lieutenants, boatswains,
gunners, pursers, carpenters, cooks), with three columns headed "persons," "how
recommended," and "how answered." This methodical arrangement is very characteristic of Pepys.

sions and patents in four volumes, compiled in the 18th century but including those in the Pepysian Collection; (5) Corbett's imposing *Collection of Precedents and Admiralty Matters, circ.* 1660–1740, in 22 volumes, including those contained in Pepys's *Navy and Admiralty Precedents* [No. 2867], but in a much later compilation; and (6) the original Survey of 1684 [MS. 97], signed by Haddock, Tippetts, and Narbrough. It should also be noted (7) that the Admiralty Library is rich in documents for the period 1660–73, where the Pepysian Collection is comparatively poor. It contains the Duke of York's *Instructions*, 4 June, 1660, to 14 March, 1673–4 [MSS. 19–22]; his *Orders*, 6 June, 1660, to 8 February, 1665–6 [MS. 23]; his *Letters*, 4 June, 1660, to 24 January, 1684–5 [MSS. 24–5]; and his *Civil Commissions and Warrants*, 8 December, 1663, to 25 February, 1684–5. It also contains (8) the *Orders of Charles II and James II* to the Principal Officers, 19 May, 1684, to 10 December, 1688 [MSS. 28, 30].

There is evidence in the Admiralty Library that Pepys left his mark upon the succeeding century as well as upon his own time. The prodigious respect paid to his authority by the naval administrators of the next generation[1]—comparable only, perhaps, to the weight which Lord Chief Justice Coke carried among the lawyers after his death—led to a number of transcripts being made from the Pepysian MSS. and preserved among the Admiralty records. Thus, (1) in a collection of papers concerning salutes, 1603–1731, some are transcribed from the Pepysian *Miscellanies*; (2) a volume of " Miscellaneous Papers on Naval Matters " includes a copy of *Naval Minutes* [No. 2866]; and (3) an important early 18th century *Naval Collection*, in three volumes bound as two, contains extracts from the *Miscellanies* with an index of all the documents not so extracted, and includes [vol. ii., p. 109] a " Catalogue of MSS.[2] and

---

(1) So durable was the tradition that the Commission which reported in June, 1805, spoke of him as "a man of extraordinary knowledge in all that related to the business" of the Navy, "of great talents, and the most indefatigable industry" (Historical MSS. Commission, *Fifteenth Report*, Appendix, pt. ii., p. 153).

(2) *cf.* Rawlinson MSS. D. 794, which contains a "List of all the official account-books and naval papers and collections belonging . . . to Samuel Pepys, as arranged by numbers upon nineteen shelves."

printed books relating to naval matters in the Pepysian Library"; (4) volume x of the Byng MSS. consists of copies of various papers in the Pepysian Library transcribed by a later hand; and (5) a register of *Memorials and Reports*, 5 September, 1674, to 19 February, 1688–9 [MS. 39], has entries in Pepys's hand, and the form of it was no doubt devised by him.[1] There is, unfortunately, no trace in the Admiralty Library of Mr. Bedford's Commonplace Book, of which volume iv. of the *Miscellanies* is a transcript.

(1) This records the " Petitioner's Name and Prayer " and the " Answers to the Prayer
by { His Majesty
     The Lords
     Mr. Pepys."

The Editor wishes to thank Mr. L. G. Carr Laughton for notes on Mountgomery's *Book of the Navy* and Edward Battine's *Method of Building Ships of War*; Mr. H. H. Brindley, of St. John's College, Cambridge, for notes on *Fragments of Ancient English Shipwrightry* and Anthony Anthony's *Declaration of the Navy*; and Mr. W. G. Perrin, the Admiralty Librarian, for facilities kindly afforded him at the Admiralty Library. He also desires most gratefully to acknowledge the unfailing kindness of Mr. Stephen Gaselee, Pepysian Librarian of Magdalene College, in allowing him access to the manuscripts at times which cannot always have been entirely convenient to himself.

J. R. TANNER.

St. John's College, Cambridge

1 October, 1913.

ABBREVIATIONS

B.M. - - - - -	British Museum.
Bodl. - - - -	Bodleian Library at Oxford.
D.N.B. - - - - -	Dictionary of National Biography (the references are to the first edition).
N.R.S. - - - -	Navy Records Society.
S.P.Dom. - - - -	State Papers Domestic.
Catalogue of Pepysian MSS. -	*A Descriptive Catalogue of the Naval Manuscripts in the Pepysian Library at Magdalene College, Cambridge* (Navy Records Society Publications, vols. xxvi, xxvii, and xxxvi, being the three volumes so far published).

"SEA" MSS.

King James II's Pocket Book . . . .

Paper, 6¼ × 3½.   pp. 30 unpaged, + 4 memo. tablets with 4 blank pp. interleaved with them.   In use, 1663–73.   Dark green morocco, with panel, richly tooled in gilt ; silver clasps ; gilt edges.

Contents.   List of ships of each rate, and also wages and salaries. Some of the pencil memoranda on the tablets are still legible.   **[488.]**

[Extracts are printed in *Catalogue of Pepysian MSS.* i. 141 (Navy Records Society's Publications, vol. xxvi.).]

Edward Fenton's Book, 1590.

Paper, 6¼ × 4½. pp. 76 unpaged, the greater part blank.   Limp brown morocco.

Contents.   Memoranda of warrants for building and repairing ships and for other naval purposes, and the assignment of moneys granted, 1588–90. There is a list of the Queen's ships at the end of the volume.   **[513.]**

[On Edward Fenton, captain and navigator, see *Dictionary of National Biography*, first edition, xviii. 320. *Cf.* also MS. No. 2133 *infra.*]

A List of His Majesty's Fleet (of his own and hired ships) employed against Holland, 1671, 1672, and 1673.   **[825.]**

[This MS. is missing.   The title is taken from Pepys's own catalogue, *Supellex Literaria*, p. 169.]

Edward Battine's Method of Building . . . Ships of War.

Paper, 7 × 4¼.   Title, dedicatory epistle, and contents + pp. 124. Dated 20 December, 1684.   Red morocco elaborately tooled ; gilt edges ; fairly written.   **[977.]**

[This MS. is fully described in *Catalogue of Pepysian MSS.* i. 230–2. There is another copy in B.M. Harl. MSS., 1283, with a dedication to Lord Dartmouth, dated 23 April, 1685.   Other MSS. are described in a paper read before the British Archæological Association by Mr. I. Chalkley Gould, entitled "Notes on a Naval Manuscript."]

B

Mr. Dummer to Mr. Pepys about improving the Art of Building Ships.

Paper, quarto. pp. 8 + double page insertion. Marbled paper covers ; fairly written, with red and black ruled borders.   **[1074.]**

[*Cf.* Bodl. Rawlinson MSS., A. 172, f. 26, "Letter to Pepys from Edmund Dummer relative to some proposals for improving the art of shipbuilding," 1 Feb., 1678-9. Edmund Dummer was assistant shipwright at Chatham. Pepys describes him early in 1686 as "an ingenious young man." See *Catalogue of Pepysian MSS.* i. 77 and 92.]

The Boke of the Lawe of Olerone : as also for the holdinge of the cowrte of the Admyrallte . . . . Per Jamys Humfrey.

Paper, quarto. pp. 415 + table of contents. Dated 1568. Standard binding, but calf instead of sheepskin ; handwriting elaborate, with marginal decorations.

Contents. p. 5, form of holding and articles of enquiry in a Court of Admiralty ; p. 25, the Laws of Oleron ; p. 49, orders for the King or Queen's ships when upon the seas in fashion of war ; p. 63, Admiral's instructions made by William Wynter, Esq., 1558, to the captains and masters of a fleet then to be transported to Portsmouth ; p. 73, articles appointed by Lord Clinton, admiral of the fleet at this present, 16 July, 1548 ; p. 79, the rates of wages in peace and war, with the expenses of officers and other charges of the Household of King Edward III, and the number of soldiers by land and sea, and of the ships retained in the wars of that King ; p. 103, the sizes of standards, banners, pennons, and guidons ; p. 108, a Declaration of an army to be made, 20 March, 1558[-9], of the Queen's and hired ships, with an estimate of the growing charge thereof. The rest of the volume contains surveys, indentures, lists, and tables of various kinds.

                                                                    [1266.]

[Pepys's own title for the work is "Jamys Humphrey's Miscellaneous Collections relating to the Admiralty and Navy of England, 1568 " (*Supellex Literaria*, p. 168). It is probably a copy of a book of Naval Collections lent to Pepys in 1668 by the Duke of York, extracts from which, some of them in Pepys's own hand, are in Bodl. Rawlinson MSS. C. 846. See also notes on *ib.* A. 233. "The Laws of Oleron" (p. 25) is a copy of a translation of "The Customs of Oleron and of the Judgments of the Sea" printed in Twiss, *The Black Book of the Admiralty* (Rolls Series), ii. 210-41, and described *ib.* pp. lxxviii-lxxxii. *Cf.* also MS. No. 2872 (*Miscellanies* iv. 515).]

An Ancient Discourse and Description of Milford Haven.

Paper, small quarto, 7¾ × 6. pp. 44 unpaged, with two large folded maps of Milford Haven inserted. Thin vellum boards.

The first map, made and coloured by hand, is dated 24 December,

38 Eliz. [1596]; the second is an engraved map, laid down by Captain Collins, and dated 1687. **[1296.]**

[The title is taken from Pepys's *Supellex Literaria* (p. 170), where the work is described as "once the Lord Burghley's book." Its contents, with several small variations, have been published from another copy in Owen's *Pembrokeshire*, Part II, London, 1897 (Cymmrodorion Record Series, No. 1). On Greenville Collins, hydrographer, see *D.N.B.* xi. 367. Another copy, but without the maps, is in MS. No. 2871 (*Miscellanies* iii. 313)].

Details of the Hampton Court, third-rate, built at Deptford by Mr. John Shish.

Paper, 7¾ × 3. ff. 17 × 2 + 63 blank pp. The Hampton Court was launched 10 July, 1678. Green morocco with panel ; gilt edges. **[1338.]**

Details of the Lennox, third-rate, built at Deptford by Mr. John Shish.

Paper, 8 × 3. ff. 50 × 2 + 11 blank pp. The Lennox was launched 12 April, 1678. Dark blue morocco ; gilt edges. **[1339.]**

An Establishment of . . Men and . . Guns.

Paper, 7¾ × 3½. pp. 28, some blank; leaves paged 1-9. Date probably 1677. Red morocco, elaborately tooled in gilt (Mearne's binding?) ; gilt edges ; fairly written. **[1340.]**

[This draft of the establishment of 1677, made by the Navy Board in pursuance of an order of the Lords of the Admiralty dated 10 March, 1673-4, is discussed, and summaries are printed, in *Catalogue of Pepysian MSS.* i. 233, and 237-41). Another copy is in Bodl. Rawlinson MSS. C. 517.]

Libellus de Policia Conceruatiua Maris.

Vellum, 7⅞ × 5¾. ff. 30, 29 lines to a page. Cent. XV. late. In paste boards covered with green and gold paper.

Collation : 1⁸-3⁸ 4⁶. **[1461.]**

Begins : Here begynnyth the prologe of the processe of the libell of englysch policie exhortyng all England to kepe the see, *etc.*

[The MS. will be found more fully described in the catalogue of *Mediæval MSS.* by Dr. M. R. James. For the printed editions of this famous poem see Gross, *Sources and Literature of English History*, p. 478.]

A Discourse touching the Current in the Strait of Gibraltar . . . . by Henry Shere.

Paper, quarto. pp. 132. Presentation copy. A letter from the author to Pepys inserted at the beginning, containing a reference to "my Journal, whereof this is almost a perfect transcript," is dated 10 March, 1674–5. Red crushed morocco, with gilt stamps; gilt edges.

An unnumbered page at the end contains four figures in illustration of pp. 7, 63, 84, and 121 of the text, and after this is inserted a letter dated Serjeant's Inn, 20 March, 1696–7, and signed "Littleton Powys," returning thanks for the loan of "a very curious tract, written with great judgment and sagacity." **[1476.]**

[Another copy is in Bodl. Rawlinson MSS., A. 341, f. 178. The "Discourse of the Mediterranean Sea and the Streights of Gibraltar," by Sir Henry Shere, or Sheeres, military engineer and author, was published in 1703 in "Miscellanies Historical and Philological, being a curious collection of private papers found in the study of a nobleman lately deceased." On Sir Littleton Powys, see *D.N.B.* xlvi. 269.]

My Diary relating to the Commission constituted by King James II, anno 1686, for the Recovery of the Navy: With a Collection of the Principal Papers incident to and conclusive of the same.

Paper, quarto. pp. 445 + table of contents. Date, *circa* 1694. Standard binding.

Contents. Documents from 1 January, 1685–6, to 8 June, 1694. **[1490.]**

[The contents of this MS. are summarised, and its bearing on naval history discussed in *Catalogue of Pepysian MSS.* i. 66-97 *Cf.* also MSS. Nos. 1534, 2823, and 2824.]

The State of the Royal Navy of England at the Dissolution of the late Commission of the Admiralty, May, 1684 . . .

Paper, small quarto. pp. 44 + index, etc. Dated 31 December, 1684. Black morocco, with elaborate gilt and blind tooling, and the royal arms on back and front—a very beautiful and striking design; gilt edges; fairly written.

Contents. In the form of a letter to the King this MS. contains a criticism of the Admiralty Commission of 14 May, 1679 to 19 May, 1684, afterwards developed by Pepys in his printed work, *Memoirs of the Royal Navy.* It is a copy of the original letter "bound as this is, and sealed up," which Pepys presented to the King, 1 January, 1684–5. **[1534.]**

[See *Catalogue of Pepysian MSS.* i. 66. *Cf.* also MSS. Nos. 1490, 2823, and 2824.]

Lieutenant Gradon's Collection of Naval Flags and Colours, 1686.

Paper, quarto. ff. 19 × 2 + index. Dark blue morocco, with panel elaborately tooled in gilt with red and yellow decoration inlaid; gilt edges.

Contents. The naval flags of various countries, illuminated in colour.
[1608.]
[John Graydon, afterwards vice-admiral, had been appointed second lieutenant of the Charles galley, 17 June, 1685. See *Catalogue of Pepysian MSS.* i. 356 and *D.N.B.* xxiii. 28.]

Nova Anglorum per mare Cronium ad Moscovitas Navigatio, authore Clemente Adam, Regiorum puerorum institutore.

Paper, quarto. pp. 116 unpaged, some blank. The account was written in 1554. Mottled sheepskin with circular ornament in gilt; gilt edges; elaborate handwriting; style that of an illuminated MS.

There is an Epistle of Dedication to Philip of Spain, headed by his coat of arms illuminated. [1663.]
[This is printed, Frankfurt, 1600, in "Marnius et Aubrius, Rerum Muscoviticarum Auctores varii". . . . *Cf.* also in Hakluyt's Collection, vol. i., "The new Navigation and discovery of the Kingdom of Moscovia by the North East, in the year 1553 . . . . performed by Richard Chancelor . . . . Written in Latin by Clement Adams." On Clement Adams, schoolmaster to the King's pages, see *D.N.B.* i. 94.]

Of Navarchi.

Paper, quarto. pp. 45 + table of contents and some blank. Thin marbled boards.

A discussion of the "shapes, sails, and other qualities" necessary to a good ship. There are some neatly drawn diagrams to illustrate the text. [1731.]
[Pepys's own title in *Supellex Literaria* (p. 171) is "A Treatise of Naval Architecture," by Mr. Fortree. It begins: "I shall not treat here of the particular art of building or framing of ships or vessels, but only of the shapes, sails, and other qualities necessary to a good sailer . . ." "Mr. Fortree" is possibly Samuel Fortree, the author of *England's Interest and Improvement, consisting in the increase of the store of trade of this Kingdom,* Cambridge, 1663.]

Mountgomery's Book of the Navy, written 1570 and 1588; with a Project for a Land Militia, addressed to King Philip, husband to Queen Mary, in the year 1557 or 1558.

Paper, quarto. pp. 31 × 2. Vellum. The dedication to the reader in verse is signed "Ber. Gar," and the text is illustrated by pen-and-ink sketches. The treatise of 1570 contains a scheme for the distribution of the Royal Navy for home defence in three squadrons on our own coasts : the appendix of 1588 gives a more detailed account of the galliasses than is easily to be found elsewhere. **[1774.]**

[" Ber. Gar" is probably Bernard Garter, the poet ; see *D.N.B.* xxi. 30. For copies in the British Museum see Add. MSS. 18035, 20042, 20043, and Arundel 22. The substance of both the original treatise of 1570 and the appendix of 1588 has been printed by Sir Samuel Brydges in *Censura Literaria*, v. 29, 137, and 260. Another copy of the " Project for a Land Militia" is in MS. No. 2869, *infra* (*Miscellanies*, i. 31).]

Mr. Hosier's Method of balancing Storekeepers' Accounts.

Paper, quarto. pp. 101 unpaged. Dated 7 November, 1668; a letter to Pepys dated 28 November, 1668, is appended. Vellum, with the royal arms in gilt ; gilt edges. **[1788.]**

[This " method" is referred to in the *Diary* under dates 6 September and 24 November, 1668, and 12 February and 7 March, 1668-9. Francis Hosier was at this time muster-master at Gravesend.]

A Collection of matters touching the Constables of Dover Castle and the Wardens of the Five Ports, gathered out of the records of the Tower and out of Lieger books of Monasteries, by Francis Thynne, Lancaster Herald.

Paper, quarto. ff. 96 × 2 + a few blank. Standard binding.

The contents include, besides the Latin text, p. 2, dedication to Henry Howard, Earl of Northampton, dated 29 July, 1604, with a pen-and-ink drawing of his arms prefixed; pp. 14–15, pen-and-ink drawings of the general arms of the Cinque Ports, and the arms of Lydd, Tenterden, Hastings, and Faversham ; p. 90, a list of the Wardens of the Cinque Ports from the reign of Edward III until 1640, with a supplementary list, 1640–85, given to Pepys by Colonel Strode. **[1811.]**

[A " Catalogue of the Lord Wardens of the Cinque Ports," by Francis Thynne, Lancaster herald, is printed in Holinshed's *Chronicles*, edition of 1808, vol. iv., pp. 810-832. Colonel Strode was Governor of Dover Castle in Pepys's time ; see *Catalogue of Pepysian MSS.* vols. ii. and iii. *passim*].

Conjectura Nautica, seu Disquisitio De Origine Navigationis.

Paper, quarto. pp. 144 unpaged, written on one side only + insertion of 12 pp. smaller size. Standard binding.

A Latin letter of dedication to Pepys from the author, Nathaniel Vincent, is prefixed. The 12 pp. inserted at the end of the volume contain

"Hadriani Beverlandi de Gigantibus Sententia" [Adrian Beverland of Middelburg]. [1825.]

[Letters from Vincent referring to this copy of his *Conjectura Nautica*, with other correspondence between them, are printed in *The Life, Journals, and Correspondence of Samuel Pepys*, i. 304, 308-21 : London, 1841.]

A Project of a form by an Order of Intrenchment for defence against a landing of any army . . . .

Paper, small folio. pp. 40 unpaged, some blank. *Temp.* Eliz.
Vellum. The Project is "directed" to Lord Burghley. [2021.]

[Another copy is in MS. No. 2871 (*Miscellanies* iii. 289).]

Instructions of the States-General of the United Provinces for the Colleges (or Courts) of Admiralty . . . .

Paper, small folio. pp. 38 unpaged, some blank. The instructions are dated 13 August, 1597. Marbled boards.

Inserted at the beginning of the volume is a letter, dated 26 March, 1678, from Thomas Bedford to Mr. Pepys, accompanying this "translation of those laws whereby the Admiralties of the States-General (although made provisionally but for a year) are still governed," and sending also for his acceptance "a short treatise written by Dr. Zouch in defence of the declining jurisdiction of the Admiralty." [2060.]

[On Richard Zouche, judge of the Court of Admiralty, see *D.N.B.* lxiii. 417. The work referred to, entitled *The Jurisdiction of the Admiralty of England asserted against Sir Edward Coke's 'Articuli Admiralitatis' in chapter xxii. of his 'Jurisdiction of Courts*,' London, 1663, is in the Pepysian library (No. 785).]

Ordres des Estats Generaux de Hollande pour maintenir en bonne Discipline leur Flottes.

Paper, small folio. pp. 28 unpaged. Dated 14 April, 1672. Marbled paper covers.

The printed Dutch original of 1672, of which this is a translation, is inserted in the middle of the volume. [2061]

A Book of all the Shipping, with their ages, names, burdens, and ordnance; as also of all Mariners, Sailors, and Fishermen, with their names, ages, and places severally . . . within the Vice-Admiralty of the South Part of Devon . . . .

Paper, folio. pp. 118 unpaged + 70 pp. blank. The list was compiled under an order from the Marquis of Buckingham, Lord High Admiral, dated 28 February, 1618[-19]. Limp vellum, with gilt tooling.
[**2122.**]

The Journals of Edward Fenton, gentleman . . . .

Paper, small folio. pp. 142 unpaged. Marbled boards, thin leather back.

Contents. (1) Voyage in the Judith as lieutenant-general and second in command to Frobisher in his third voyage to Meta Incognita, 25 May, 1578, to 17 Oct., 1578. (2) Voyage as admiral in the Bear galleon (afterwards called the Leicester), 29 April, 1582, to 2 July, 1583. (3) A small sheet containing a form of prayer is inserted at the beginning of the volume and two memoranda at the end. [**2133.**]

[*Cf.* MS. No. 513 *supra*. An account of the 'voyage intended towards China,' on which Fenton went as admiral in the Bear, written by Luke Ward, his vice-admiral, is in Hakluyt's *Principal Voyages of the English Nation. Cf.* also B. M. Cott. MSS. Otho E viii. ff. 135-9, 162, 163, 177, 201, and Titus B viii. 171].

A Report from a Commission of Enquiry held in the Beginning of King James I touching the then Abuses and Corruptions of the Navy, and proper Remedies applicable thereto.

Paper, small folio. pp. 166 + some blank. Standard binding.

This is a copy of the Report of the Commission of 1608.

[**2165.**]

[A copy of this Report is in S. P. Dom. Jac. I. xli., and the depositions on which it was based are in Cott. MSS. Julius F iii. (See Oppenheim, *The Administration of the Royal Navy*, p. 193*n*). Another copy under a different title is in MS. No. 2871 (*Miscellanies* iii. 355).]

Mr. Flamsteed's Account of the Beginning, Progress, and present State of our Improvements and Deficiencies in the Doctrine and Practice of Navigation.

Paper, small folio. ff. 24 × 2 + 32 unpaged. Dated 21 April, 1697. Thin art boards.

The contents are in the form of a letter to Pepys arising out of his request for "an account of what improvements the art of navigation may probably receive from such seminaries of well-educated seamen as that . . . . at Christ's Hospital." This led to further correspondence, the original letters being bound up in the volume. **[2184.]**

[A transcript from this MS. is in B.M. Add. MSS. 30221. On John Flamsteed, first astronomer royal, see *D.N.B.* xix. 241.]

Papers of Mr. Halley's and the learned Mr. Greaves's, touching our yet imperfect Attainments in the Art of Navigation : with notes subsequent thereto.

Paper, small folio. pp. 34 unpaged. Mr. Halley's paper is dated 17 February, 1695-6. Mr. Greaves's papers are *circ.* 1640. Art boards.

The contents include a letter from Mr. Hunter, dated 3 July, 1696, "upon information taken by him from the gentlemen of the Trinity House," referring to errors in navigation made by the fleet two days after the battle of Southwold Bay, May, 1672, and by Lord Sandwich on his return from the Sound with a squadron in 1659. **[2185.]**

[A transcript from this MS. is in B.M. Add. MSS. 30221. On Edmund Halley the astronomer, see *D.N.B.* xxiv. 104 ; on John Greaves the mathematician, see *ib.* xxiii, 38.]

Mr. Holland his First Discourse of the Navy written Anno 1638.

Paper, folio. pp. 164 (only 122 paged). Standard binding, but slightly varied with panel.

To John Hollond's "First Discourse," dated (in pencil) 29 September, 1638, is appended a copy of Slyngesbie's "Discourse" of the Navy (1660), but this is not dated or attributed to any author. **[2193.]**

[These Discourses have been printed for the Navy Records Society (Publications, vol. vii.), together with Hollond's "Second Discourse" (MS. No. 2835 *infra*). The principal extant MSS. of the "First Discourse" are described on p. lxviii. of this volume, and those of Slyngesbie's "Discourse" on p. lxxxii. Another copy of the latter is in MS. No. 2871 (*Miscellanies* iii. 683).]

Extracts from the . . . . four most ancient Council-Books . . . . relating principally to the then Marine Affairs of England . . . .

Paper, folio. pp. xxxiv. + 62. Art paper boards.

Contents. pp. i.–xiii., 8 Oct., 1541—22 July, 1543 ; pp. xv.–xxxiv., 31 Jan., 1546[-7]—4 Oct., 1549; pp. 1–27, 6 Oct., 1549—29 June, 1551 ; pp. 29–54, 3 July, 1551—16 June, 1553 ; pp. 55–62, table of contents. The entries on pp. xv.–54 are described as "taken from the

Lord Clarendon's copy thereof transcribed and examined from the
original by Garter King [and] Rouge Dragon, 1680-1."   **[2197.]**

Balfour's Practiques . . . . .

   Paper, folio.   pp. 8 unpaged (table of contents) + pp. 471 × 2
paged + pp. 32 unpaged.   *Temp.* Eliz.   Standard binding.

   " Presented to the Duke of Lauderdale by his Grace's humble servant
Geo. Mackenzie, 14 December, 1676," is written above Pepys's book-
plate by a hand much later than that of the text.   **[2208.]**

[Balfour's "Practicks," ascribed to Sir James Balfour of Pittendreich, who died in 1583,
is the earliest text-book of Scottish law.   It was not printed until 1754.]

Collectiones Trevorianae . . . . .

   Paper, folio.   pp. 949 + 16 pp. unpaged.   Standard binding.

   The contents consist of " particular select heads, transcribed from the
more copious common-place book of historical notes taken from records
by the learned Arthur Trevor, and lent me (with other like MSS., papers
of his) by my honoured friend Sir John Trevor, in favour of my naval
enquiries, etc."   There is added at the end of the volume " An alphabet
of such of the titles in Arthur Trevor's general common-place book as
are not taken notice of in this Collection ; but may upon occasion be
resorted to from the book itself in the hands of Sir John Trevor." **[2217.]**

[MS. No. 2829 *infra* is a transcript of the Index to the Trevor papers.]

An Abstract of a Declaration of the Navy Royal of England . . . . by
Anthony Anthony . . . .

   Paper, 9½ × 11¾.   ff. 10 paper + ff. 20 two thicknesses of thin pasteboard.   The original rolls are dated 1546 : this may be an abstract made
for Pepys.   Oblong mottled sheepskin with inlaid panel ; brass clasps
(one broken) ; gilt edges.

   Contents.   Illuminations of three " pinnaces," three " row-barges," six
" galliasses," and five " ships," with their tonnage and number of men.
                                                           [2219.]

[*Cf.* MS. No. 2991 *infra*, which contains part of the original " Declaration."]

Collections touching the present Government and Force of the Navy of
France, by Sir Anthony Deane at his being there . . . . Anno 1675.

Paper, folio. pp. 34, some blank. Marbled boards, much broken.
[2241.]

[Sir Anthony Deane, the famous shipbuilder, visited France in 1675 to superintend the delivery of the two yachts which he had built for Louis XIV (*Catalogue of Pepysian MSS.* iii. 83)].

S.P.'s Address to the Duke of York, 20 August, 1668, with his Royal Highness's proceedings upon the same.

Paper, folio. pp. 144. Dark blue morocco with panel; gilt edges.
[2242.]

[This MS. is fully discussed in *Catalogue of Pepysian MSS.* i. 28 -36. Pepys's Diary of the whole proceedings is also to be found in MS. No. 2874 *infra* (*Miscellanies*, vi. 385–504). See also *Diary*, 20 Aug.–13 Sept., 1668].

Abstract of Naval Papers collected for the Parliament.

Two portfolios of miscellaneous original papers bound up together. The documents in vol. i. are numbered 1–107; those in vol. ii., 108–218; but Nos. 6, 85, 179 and 180 are wanting; 24 pp. table of contents for both volumes is prefixed to vol. i. Brown paper boards; quarter-sheep; with portfolio strings attached. [2265 and 2266.]

Contents. Largely surveys, estimates, and other papers bearing on naval finance, 1660–79, and on the preparations for war with France in 1678; but the collection appears to contain all the papers at any time called for by and presented to Parliament during Pepys's tenure of office, as far as the end of his first Secretaryship of the Admiralty in 1679. The following are the more important of them :

Volume I [2265]

No. 1.—The debt of the navy estimated by the officers of the navy in several years from 1643 to 1660.

No. 2.—An abstract shewing the number, rate, quality, beginning, and ending of every ship and vessel of his Majesty's from the year 1600 to this 20th of February, 1676-7.

No. 4.—A short account of the naval action of England in reference to peace and war, from the determination of the first Dutch war, anno 1654, to this present October, 1675.

No. 8—An estimate of the present debts of his Majesty's navy to the 27th June last 1660 [dated 9th August, 1660].

No. 12.—Abstract of the tons, men, and guns of the two fleets of anno 1660 and 1676 compared.

No. 13.—An abstract of the distinct numbers and force of the present fleets of England, France, and Holland, consisting of 20 guns and upwards, October, 1675; and a list of the English, French, and Dutch fleets.
[*Cf.* No. 70 below. Other copies are No. 162 below and in MS. No. 2873 (*Miscellanies*, v. 198). Printed in *Catalogue of Pepysian MSS.* i. 46.]

No. 15.—Report of the officers of the navy upon several queries made by the Lord High Admiral touching the state of the navy, its stores, debt, etc., January, 1661[–2].

No. 19.—Merchant-ships hired to serve as men-of-war in the first Dutch War, 1652-3, and in the second Dutch war, 1665-7.

No. 21.—Instances of the great burdens and force of ships of the French and Dutch.

No. 27.—The charge of building a ship of each rate in his Majesty's yards compared with the price of the like ships built by contract; as also a computation of the number of workmen of each distinct sort needful for the building of a ship of each rate in 12 months. November, 1675.

No. 35.—A particular of all the docks and slips within this his Majesty's kingdom at this day, in or upon which 1st, 2nd, and 3rd rate ships may be built. As also a list of the master-shipwrights in England judged of present sufficiency to be intrusted with the building of 1st, 2nd, and 3rd rate ships. [1675?]

No. 37.—Charge of the navy for the year 1676.

No. 39.—Notes relating to the measures of my computation of the charge of building twenty ships [1675?].

No. 40.—Several representations from the commissioners of the admiralty of the ill state of the concernments of the navy just before his Majesty's restoration, 1659 and 1660.

No. 42.—Observations touching contract-ships' defects; and further notes about contract-ships [from 1652 to 1668].
[*Cf.* Hollond, *Discourses of the Navy*, pp. 29-44 (*N.R.S.* Publications, vol. vii).]

No. 44.—Report from the officers of the ordnance, shewing the yearly expense, receipts, and present debt of their office (relating to the service of the navy only), from the King's restoration to this day [18th May, 1675]. . . .

No. 47.—An abstract of the debt of the navy as it was in 1660, 1667, 1672, 1673, 1675.

No. 48.—A list of French ships and galleys [1674].

No. 50.—A list of the King's ships, with a report on 'the general state of the navy', 12th Dec., 1642.

No. 51.—Contract with Mr. Castle about repairing the Crown and Dover, 17th November, 1670.

No. 52.—An abstract of the prices given by the officers of the navy for several of the principal stores used therein from 1668 to 1675.

No. 53.—Number of shipwrights and their servants employed in his Majesty's yards in the years 1666 and 1667.

No. 55.—The Lord Treasurer's virtues in his payments [*shorthand*].

No. 56.—The state of the Forest of Dean, given in by the officers of the navy : taken 1671.

No. 58.—Notes taken by discourse at the navy office about our want and building of ships, February 20th, 1676.

No. 62.—Mr. Tippetts and Commissioner Deane their report about the number of shipwrights and other workmen necessary to build a ship of the 1st, 2nd, and 3rd rate in a 12 months' time; number of shipwrights and caulkers in this kingdom, with the places of their residence; their opinion of the number of men and time the repair of the King's fleet will take up to finish the same. May 16th, 1675.

Nos. 63–6, 71–2, 97.—Papers relating to the proposal for building twenty new ships, 1674-5.
[See *Catalogue of Pepysian MSS.* i. 42-8.]

No. 70.—An abstract of the distinct numbers and force of the present fleets of England, France, and Holland consisting of 20 guns and upwards.
[*Cf.* No. 13 above and No. 162 below.]

No. 88.—The present fleets of English, French, and Dutch, 1673.

No. 92.—Ships built by the King of France since anno 1672.

No. 102.—Copy of Sir William Coventry's proposal for reducing the charge of the navy of £200,000 a year, with the navy board's letter relating to it. 29th August, 1667. [*Cf.* also No. 104.]
[See *Catalogue of Pepysian MSS.* i. 104.]

No. 103.—Account of the condition of his Majesty's affairs of the navy from 14th July, 1673 (the date of the present commission of the admiralty) to 28th January, 1673[-4].

No. 105.—A list of the French fleet, 1676.

Volume II [2266]

No. 108.—The number of shipwrights in England, 31st January, 1676-7.

Nos. 109–114, 116, 127-8, 130-1, 206, 208-9.—Papers relating to the building of thirty new ships [1679].
[See *Catalogue of Pepysian MSS.* i. 48-55, 223. *Cf.* Bodl. Rawlinson MSS. A. 185, ff. 161-3.]

No. 115.—An answer given me this morning [7th April, 1677] by Sir John Tippetts, surveyor of the navy, to a question I by discourse lately committed to his considering, viz. : What is the best naval force that can be set to sea in the least time in case his Majesty's service should require it? Occasioned by the late addresses to the King from the two Houses of Parliament against the growth of France.

No. 119.—Notes for discourse in Parliament introductory to the debate of the business of the navy, 22 Oct., 1675.
[See *Catalogue of Pepysian MSS.* i. 47 and *cf.* MS. No. 2870 (*Miscellanies* ii. 453).]

Nos. 120-1, 126, 129, 133-5, 138, 142, 145, 165-205, 210-215.—Papers relating to the proposed fleet of 90 ships [1678].
[See *Catalogue of Pepysian MSS.* i. 55. *Cf.* Bodl. Rawlinson MSS. A. 176, ff. 1, 3, 4, 10, 17-19, 98.]

No. 123.—An abstract of the number of men-of-war, fireships, tenders, victuallers, etc., employed in the last war in 1673, with the number of men employed therein.

No. 136.—Moneys paid for sick and wounded, anno 1672 and 1673.
[*Cf*. MS. No. 2874 (*Miscellanies* vi. 47).]

No. 137.—The charge his Majesty was at by his royal bounty given to the relations of persons slain in his service at sea during the last war with the Dutch, January 15th, 1677-8.

No. 147.—Charges extraordinary relating to the head of wages which attend a war, over and above what is provided for in the ordinary book of rates.

No. 148.—The proportion of able seamen to ordinary, as his Majesty's ships must be manned fit for service : by Sir Anthony Deane.

No. 151.—The report this day [11th October, 1666] made and agreed to by the House of Commons from Sir William Lowther, chairman to the committee for inspecting the accounts of the navy during the late naval war with Holland. Given me by Sir William Lowther this 8th February, 1677[-8].

No. 152.—A copy given me by Sir William Lowther, February, 1677[-8], of the report from the committees appointed to inspect the several accounts of the navy, ordnance, and stores made to the House (*vid*. the extract of the House's Journal) the 11th of October, 1666.

No. 153.—An extract of the journal of the House of Commons relating to the committee appointed for inspecting the accounts of the navy for the late war with Holland, with the said committee's report thereon. In which report £4 per man a month is admitted by the Parliament itself by their agreement with the said committee for the medium of the navy charge without ordnance : September and October, 1666.

No. 154.—[7th February, 1677-8] A list of the committee for inspecting the master of the ordnance and secretary of the admiralty's papers, with a note on such thereof as were of the committee for inspecting the accounts of the navy after the Dutch War, anno 1666, with a list of the said last committee : September 26th, 1666.

No. 155.—Report of the committee for inspecting the master of the ordnance and secretary of the admiralty's papers, wherein the sum allowed for the charge of a naval war is calculated by the medium of £4. 5. per man a month, the ordnance included : February 12th, 1677-8.

No. 162.—An abstract of the distinct numbers and force of the present fleets of England, France, and Holland, consisting of 20 guns and upwards.
[*Cf*. No. 70 above. Other copies are No. 13 above and in MS. No. 2873 (*Miscellanies* v. 198).]

No. 163.—Ships built by the French since anno 1678, and the King of France's great works done towards the advancement of his navy at Toulon, Brest, Marseilles, Havre de Grâce, and since that time.

No. 216.—The naval force of England anno 1660 and anno 1678 compared, as to their number, sorts, tonnage, guns, men.

Libro de Cargos : de Bastimentos y municiones que se hazen a los cappitanes y maestres y patrones de las naves y otres navios que sirven en el Armada de su magestad este anno de MDLXXXVII siendo proveedor della Bernabe de Pedroso.

Paper, folio. pp. 556 unpaged, many blank. Vellum boards, backed with calf; much worn.   The book is pierced with a large hole, probably for convenience of hanging up on board ship.

Contents.   A list of the victuals and supplies belonging to the captains of the ships serving in the Spanish fleet, 1587, the contractor being Bernabe de Pedroso.   The names of each captain and his ship occur at the head of the page, with a list of stores and their quantities below —biscuits, wine, bacon, tunny, pease, vinegar, oil, cheese, water; also lists of various utensils such as pots, dishes, measures, etc.   **[2269.]**

[Pepys's own title in *Supellex Literaria* (p. 167) is "The Original Libro de Cargos (as to provisions and munition) of the Proveedor-General of the Spanish Armada, 1588".)

Notes towards a right judgment touching the present Mediterranean Expedition.

Paper, folio.   pp. 42 unpaged, but the paragraphs are numbered in pencil in the margin.   Dated 31 January, 1694–5.   Plain boards.

Contents.   A criticism of Admiral Russell's expedition to the Mediterranean of June, 1694.   Inserted opposite § 24 is a sheet of paper containing a summary of the arguments with notes in shorthand. At the end is copied an unsigned letter headed "Reflections on Mr. R——'s voyage to the Mediterranean in a letter to a Friend."

[2276.]

John Cox his Travels over the Land into the South Seas, and from thence round the South part of America to Barbados and Antigo.

Paper, folio.   pp. 166 unpaged, some blank; written on right-hand page only.   Calf with panel; gilt edges; portfolio fastenings. The journal is from 5 April, 1680, to 31 Jan., 1681[–2].   **[2349.]**

Sir Richard Munden's and Thomas Willshaw's Journals.

Paper, folio.   pp. 116, some blank.   Marbled boards with leather back; gilt edges.

Sir Richard Munden's Journal, 12 Jan., 1672–3, to 12 Sept., 1673, "relating to his retaking St. Helena and taking the Dutch East India ships" is written on the left-hand page as far as 5 May, and then on both pages.   The Journal of Thomas Willshaw, commander of the Castle Frigate fireship, in his voyage to St. Helena, from 15 Jan., 1672–3, is on the right-hand page only, and ends at 5 May, 1673.   Appended

is a letter from Richard Gibson to Pepys, dated 7 April, 1683, criticising
Sir Richard Munden's proceedings.   [**2350.**]

[Mr. Richard Gibson is frequently referred to in Pepys's *Admiralty Letters;* see
Catalogue of Pepysian MSS. vols. ii. and iii. indexes. MS. No. 2543 is another
copy of Munden's Journal.]

A Collection of Sea Journals of several Commanders and Lieutenants of
his Majesty's ships, abstracted and compared (with useful reflections made
thereon) by Mr. Gibson, 1684.

Paper, folio. pp. 200 unpaged, some blank, + two insertions of 4 pp.
each. Marbled paper boards ; leather back.

Some of the abstracts here given were originally folded twice and
endorsed on the back ; they are now bound into the volume.   [**2351.**]

[On Mr. Richard Gibson see note to No. 2350 *supra.*]

A Collection of Extracts Naval out of the Latin-English Historians and
French within-named.

Paper, folio. 2 pp. table of contents + 8 pp. paged A to H + 761 pp.
+ 5 blank. Standard binding.   [**2363.**]

Mr. Deane's Method of measuring the Body of a Ship and pre-calculating
her Draught of Water.

Paper, folio. pp. 18. Marbled paper covers, much worn.

Contents. Section drawings of a ship's body, with calculations. [**2501.**]

['Mr. Deane' is Sir Anthony Deane, the famous shipbuilder. He was knighted in
1675.]

A Relation of a Voyage for the Discovery of a Passage by the North East
to Japan and China, performed in his Majesty's ship the Speedwell and
the Prosperous pink ... 1676 : .... With some good observations ...
by Captain John Wood.

Paper, folio. pp. 90 unpaged, many blank. Vellum, with gilt-tooled
panel ; gilt edges.

Two maps are inserted at the beginning, and a quarto tract by Moxon
on the same subject is bound up in the volume.   [**2542.**]

[Another copy is in Bodl. Rawlinson MSS., A. 467. Printed in Narbrough's *Voyages*,
London, 1694, pp. 143-196. See also *Catalogue of Pepysian MSS.* vol. iii. p. xxiv *n.*]

Journal of the ship Assistance by Sir Richard Munden, 1672–3.

Paper, folio. pp. 160 unpaged, many blank ; writing on right-hand page only. Vellum, backed with thin calf ; remains of portfolio fastenings.

The journal is from Sunday, 12 January, 1672–3, to Friday, 12 September, 1673. Opposite the entry for Tuesday, 6 May, is inserted a coloured drawing to illustrate the surrender of St. Helena on the previous day ; a map is also inserted at the end of the written pages. [See also MS. No. 2350 *supra.*] [**2543.**]

Mr. Pepys's Defence . . . of the Conduct of the Navy . . . during the late War with Holland . . .

Paper, folio. pp. 160 unpaged. Dated 1669–70. Mottled calf with plain panel.

To a copy of the whole proceedings is appended the original of the greater part of them—" the foregoing General Defence as delivered by Mr. Pepys, November 29, read December 14, and sworn to by him before " the Commissioners appointed by Parliament for inspecting the accounts of the war, " and that attested by their then Chairman (Giles Dunster, merchant), January 12, 1669[–70]: refallen into his own hands upon the determination of the Commission." [**2554.**]

[This document is fully discussed in *Catalogue of Pepysian MSS.* i. 33–6 ; see also p. 143. Other copies are in MS. No. 2874 *infra* (*Miscellanies*, vi. 509–581) and Bodl. Rawlinson MSS. A. 457].

A Journal kept on board his Majesty's ship Prince by Captain John Narbrough, lieutenant for this expedition on board the Prince.

Paper, folio. pp. 286 unpaged, a large part blank. Vellum boards backed with thin calf ; remains of portfolio fastenings.

The journal is from 7 Jan., 1671–2, to 18 Sept., 1672. [**2555.**]

[A copy is in MS. No. 2869 (*Miscellanies* i. 221.]

Journals kept by John Narbrough as Commander of his Majesty's Ship Fairfax in her voyage to Spain and as Captain of his Majesty's Ship St. Michael on her voyage to the Northward.

Paper, folio. pp. 204 unpaged, some blank. Vellum boards, backed with thin calf ; remains of portfolio fastenings.

The journal on board the Fairfax is from 18 Sept., 1672, to 1 July, 1673 ; that on board the St. Michael is from 1 July, 1673, to 21 Sept., 1673. The text is illustrated by charts and coloured drawings. [**2556.**]

C

Navy White Book.

Paper, folio.   pp. 276 + pp. 8 ledger index.   Vellum, with panel and royal arms.

Contents.   P. 1 : Notes in shorthand relating mainly to abuses in the navy, 5 Jan., 1663–4, to 25 July, 1667; p. 101, Memorandum of 23 Jan., 1666–7, relating to victuals at Livorne; p. 102, "Objections against Mr. Wells's proposal of his having all his Majesty's old cordage above 5 inches, and all bolt-ropes, and in lieu thereof to ease the King of all charge in port-rope, netting-rope, lashing line, and black oakum "; p. 103, "A collection of loose notes which I had occasionally taken in shorthand (most of them within the time of the late war) containing matters for future reflection"; these are notes, written in longhand, mainly on abuses from 23 Aug., 1666, to 31 Aug., 1668 ; pp. 122–end, Miscellaneous private notes and memoranda of a similar kind, from 1 Dec., 1668, to Dec., 1672.   **[2581.]**

Instructions to Commissioners, and Journals relating to Virginia, 1676–7.

Paper, folio.   pp. 250 unpaged, some blank, and 8 pp. insertion at the end.   Vellum, backed with thin sheepskin ; the usual arms and gilt tooling are omitted.   **[2582.]**

[A full list of the contents of this volume is given in Andrews and Davenport, *Guide to the Manuscript Materials for the History of the United States to 1783* (Carnegie Institute of Washington, 1908), pp. 425–8.]

Naval Accounts, 1667 and 1668.

Paper, folio.   pp. 220 unpaged, some blank.   Vellum, with gilt tooled panel.

Contents.   Printed forms with figures filled in, giving a weekly abstract of accounts from 31 December, 1667, to 31 December, 1668.
                                                                          [2583.]

Benjamin Waters's Journal of a Voyage towards Bantam.

Paper, folio.   pp. 136 unpaged, many blank.   Mottled calf with plain panel.

Contents.   Journal of the Voyage of Benjamin Waters, a mate in the employ of the East India Company, in the Formosa, Captain James Marriner, commander, first "from Swally Marine towards Bantam," Tuesday, 20 March, 1676–7, to Saturday, 2 June, 1677 ; thence "to

Eymoy upon the coast of China," Tuesday, 12 June, 1677, to Sunday, 15 July, 1677; thence back again to Bantam, Monday, 24 December, 1677, to Friday, 11 January, 1677–8. Also in the Anne, Captain Zachary Browne, commander, from Java Head to the Downs, Sunday, 3 February, 1677–8, to Wednesday, 31 July, 1678. A dedication to Charles II is prefixed, and tables of the courses steered, soundings, and the bearings of the land are appended. [2584.]

Collections towards the stating the expense of his Majesty's Navy from the beginning of the present war, and more especially for the justifying the account thereof presented to the Parliament at their Session begun 18 September, 1666.

Paper, folio. pp. 160 + a few blank. Dark blue morocco with gilt tooled panel; royal arms; gilt edges. [2589.]

[This MS. is discussed in *Catalogue of Pepysian MS.* i. 100.]

Captain Bartholomew Sharpe's Journal of a South Sea Voyage.

Paper, folio. pp. 40 blank unpaged + pp. 97 × 2 + pp. 45 blank unpaged; written and paged on the right hand only. Quarter sheepskin with vellum boards; portfolio fastenings.

Contents. P. 1: Journal in the South Seas, 5 Apr., 1680, to 28 June, 1681. P. 62: Journal from the Gulf of A Dulce (Golfo Dulce) on the coast of Reco (Arica) to the South, 29 June, 1681, to 28 Jan., 1681–2. [2610.]

[On Captain Bartholomew Sharpe, see *D.N.B.* li. 419. Two copies of the Journal are in B.M., Sloane MSS. 46, and others in the Admiralty Library and in MS. No. 2874 (*Miscellanies*, vi. 271, 333). *Cf.* also Hacke's *Voyages*, London, 1699.]

Penn's Naval Collections.

Paper, folio. ff. paged as 1–112, 193–212, 113–192, 213–246 + table of contents, index, and some blank pages. The dedication to the King is dated 22 June, 1680. Red morocco, with gilt-tooled panel and royal arms; gilt edges.

Contents. "A collection of several manuscripts taken out of Sir William Penn's closet relating to the affairs of the Navy, humbly dedicated and presented to the King by his son William Penn": p. 1, Instructions given by George, Marquis of Buckingham, Lord High Admiral of England, for the government of the navy; p. 65, The

office of the Admiralty of England in the reign of King Charles I. . . .
p. 95, Instructions for the Admiralty by the Lords and Commons in
Parliament, anno 1647; p. 193, Discourse of the well-governing of
the Navy about the year 1649; p. 113, The establishment of the
Admiralty and Navy by King Charles II., anno. 1660; p. 213,
A collection of orders and instructions for several services by the
Generals and Admirals of the Fleet during the late rebellion, with
some additions made thereto by Sir William Penn when he com-
manded under the Duke [of York], 1664 and 1665, containing
instructions for prizes, 1653, for sailing, 1664, for chasing, 1665, for
fighting, 1653, for punishing offenders, 1653, and a memorandum of
Penn's, addressed to Sir William Coventry, on the duties of a commander
at sea.   [2611.]
[Another copy of p. 113 is in MS. No. 2867 (*Naval Precedents*, p. 350) and it is printed
in Penn, *Life of Sir William Penn*, ii. 243–5. On p. 213 see Corbett, *Fighting
Instructions*, 1530–1816, pp. 99, 129. *Cf.* also the Penn Papers, B.M. Sloane MSS.
3232, where a copy of Buckingham's Instructions occurs.]

Bibliotheca Nautica, 1695 . . . .

Paper, folio. pp. 94, some of them small folio inserted. Marbled
boards.

Contents. "Catalogues of authors . . . . upon the art and practice of
Navigation, collected chiefly as to Portuguese and Spanish from
D. Nicolao Antonio and D. Antonio de Leon; as to Dutch, from
Mr. Joseph Hill of Rotterdam; as to French, from Le Sieur De la
Croix-du-Maine; as to English, from all that appears to have been ever
hitherto printed touching Navigation, Shipwrightry, Boatswainry, or
Pilotage in our own language: with a chronological catalogue of the
most eminent mathematicians of this nation (ancient and modern) to
the year 1673."   [2643.]

Captain Robert Holmes his Journals of two voyages into Guinea in his
Majesty's ships the Henrietta and the Jersey in the years 1660-1 and
1663-4.

Paper, folio. pp. 266 unpaged, many blank. Vellum with red label
at back ; and ties.

Contents. (1) Journal in the Henrietta, 2 November, 1660, to 28 July,
1661 ; (2) Soundings at the mouth of the river of Gambia, 9 March,
1660-1 ; (3) Miscellaneous 'letters, instructions, and results' relating to
the voyage ; (4) Journal in the Jersey, 21 November, 1663, to 3 January,
1664-5 ; (5) Miscellaneous letters and papers relating to the voyage.
                                                                 [2698.]

A Catalogue to Mr. Pepys's books on Navigation.

Paper, folio.   pp. 6 unpaged + 81.   Marbled boards.

Contents.   "A Catalogue and Alphabet to my Books of Geography and Hydrography . . . . resting in my Library at its adjustment, Midsummer, 1693, and from thence by additions carried on to Midsummer, 1695, and from thence by further additions to the completion of the Library." The Catalogue has numerous interlineations and corrections.   **[2700.]**

Extracts Marine and Naval collected out of . . . . English Historians.

Paper, folio.   pp. 184.   Standard binding; leather torn.

Contents.   An index of references to the following : p. 1, Holinshed's Chronicle vol. i. ; p. 13, Holinshed's Chronicle, vol ii.; p. 37, Speed's Chronicle ; p. 61, Speed's History of Great Britain ; p. 93, Caxton's Chronicle ; p. 101, Fabyan's Chronicle; p. 113, Stow's Chronicle ; p. 137, Daniel and Trussell's Chronicle ; p. 149, Baker's Chronicle ; p. 169, Dugdale's Baronage ; p. 177, Froissart's Chronicle.   **[2714.]**

Two Naval Papers . . . . with a report of Mr. Pepys's, 1669.   **[2735]**

Paper, folio.   pp. 112.   Dark blue morocco, with panel; gilt edges.

Contents.   p. 1, "A Project for contracting the charge of his Majesty's Navy, keeping the coasts of England and Ireland safely guarded, and his Majesty's ships in harbour sufficiently secured as now they are, provided that the old debts be paid, the provisions hereunder-mentioned supplied, and a certain assignment settled for the future payment of the Navy quarterly, wrote by the Earl of Nottingham, Lord High Admiral of England, and the Principal Officers of the Navy"; followed by "the particular directions for putting this project in execution," in the form of instructions to the storekeepers and other dockyard officials. The various memoranda and instructions are initialled by Sir Robert Mansell, Sir Guilford Slingsby, Sir Richard Bingley, and Peter Buck, as Principal Officers of the Navy.

[*Cf.* MS. No. 2870 (*Miscellanies* ii. 133).   The 'project,' although without the 'particular directions,' is printed in Charnock, *Marine Architecture*, ii. 184-196]

P. 44, Propositions for regulating the Navy, A.D. 1618.

[This is a copy of the Report of the Special Commission appointed 23 June, 1618, to enquire into the abuses of the Navy. A memorandum on p. 47, signed by Pepys, records "that the original books of Propositions above-mentioned . . . . remain in the Paper Office in the custody of Joseph Williamson, Esq., where he lately gave me the perusal of them, and of which Sir William Coventry having heretofore taken copies, and from thence procured the following transcripts." *Cf.* S. P. Dom. Jac. I., vols. c. and ci., and Bodl. Rawlinson MSS. A. 192, f. 12 ; 215, f. 252 ; 455, 458, 459. See also *Diary*, 14 and 17 Mar., 1668-9. The report is printed, but not very accurately, in Charnock, *Marine Architecture* ii. 211-70, and extracts from pp. 83-4 are also given in Derrick, *Memoirs of the Royal Navy*, pp. 52-3. For an account of the reorganisation of 1618, see Oppenheim, *The Administration of the Royal Navy*, p. 194].

P. 110 : Mr. Pepys's Report touching the ancient and present Œconomy of the Navy of England under the Lord High Admiral, presented from the Navy Board to his Royal Highness the Duke of York (then Admiral), 17 April, 1669.

[This is in the form of a joint letter to the Duke of York, signed by Lord Brouncker, Sir John Mennes, Thomas Middleton, Samuel Pepys, and John Cox, giving a brief account, in pursuance of the Duke's commands, of the administration of the Navy Office ; it refers to various documents originally annexed, to which it served as a covering letter. It is printed in Charnock, *Marine Architecture*, ii. 404-8.]

A General List of the Names of Persons this Day [1 Jan., 1686-7] in Employment in the Admiralty and Royal Navy ; with the nature of their several Employments therein.

Paper, folio. pp. 28. Marbled boards. This contains, in addition to the established offices, the names of commanders and masters on half-pay, "persons enjoying pensions," "clerks and other instruments," and warrant officers belonging to each ship.   [2762.]

A Discourse concerning the Spanish Fleet invading England in the year 1588 . . . . written in Italian by Petruccio Ubaldino, citizen of Florence.

Paper, folio. pp. 21 + engraved title-page and 11 engraved maps drawn by Robert Adams ; also 6 loose pages with an index to the maps and text under dates. Standard binding.

The dedications to Lord Howard of Effingham and to the reader are both in the name of Augustine Ryther, the engraver of the maps, who refers to the book as "kept back these two years almost from our men in an unknown tongue," "translated and printed at my cost," and "by my friend translated faithfully, only the Italian flourishes were here and there omitted, because in our English tongue they could not sound well without suspicion of flattery."   [2806.]

[The work is a translation, published by Ryther in 1590, of Petruccio Ubaldini's " Expeditionis Hispaniorum in Angliam vera Descriptio." It was reprinted in 1740, with the omission of the " Epistle to the Reader," under the title " A Genuine and most Impartial Narration of the Glorious Victory obtained by her Majesty's Navy . . .

over the falsely styled invincible Armada of Spain, A.D. 1588." A copy of Ryther's edition of 1590 is in the Pepysian Library, bound up in vol. i. of *Sea Tracts* (No. 1077, p. 907). On Augustine Ryther see *D.N.B.* 1. 69, and on Robert Adams, *ib.* i. 100. On the maps see Lowndes, *Bibliographer's Manual*, p. 2465.]

A Journal of my Voyage from England to Newfoundland and the Straits in his Majesty's ship Leopard under the command of Sir William Poole, Knight. [By Benjamin Poole, second lieutenant of the Leopard].

Paper, folio. pp. 92 unpaged, many blank. Vellum ; gilt edges.

The Journal is from 27 March, 1677, to 5 June, 1678.   **[2813.]**

Fragments of Ancient English Shipwrightry.

Paper, folio. pp. 56 + pp. 28 double pasteboard + pp. 78 + pp. 96 blank, all unpaged. Calf. Probably belongs to the period 1570–1620.

Curious and interesting. The drawings are delicate, and some of them are coloured.   **[2820.]**

[The title is taken from Pepys's *Supellex Literaria* (p. 171), as the work is without one, but the instructions for laying out the tables of dimensions, and the full series of moulds, together with the statements of materials, show that 'Fragments' is scarcely an appreciative description. The work should be compared with Sutherland's *Shipbuilder's Assistant* (1711), the 18th century classic on the subject of building and rigging. From the rigging of the single large vessel which is sketched, masted and rigged, on an early page, and from the large scale coloured sketches of hulls, it appears probable that the work falls between 1570 and 1620. The drawings of figures at the beginning of the volume appear to be of the same date as the rest of the work, but the artist must have had in mind the style of the miniaturists of a century or more earlier. The sketch of the ship-designer and his assistant in a mould-loft is of special interest.]

Report of the Special Commission appointed 17 April, 1686, on their first year's proceedings, ending at Lady Day, 1687, dated 11 Aug., 1687.

Paper, folio. pp. 46 unpaged, a few blank. Marbled boards ; gilt edges.

The signatures of the Commissioners are original, and possibly the Report itself.   **[2823.]**

[*Cf.* Pepys's *Memoirs of the Royal Navy;* MSS. Nos. 1490 and 1534 *supra;* MS. No. 2824 *infra*].

Report of the Special Commission appointed 17 April, 1686, on their second year's proceedings, ending at Lady Day, 1688, dated 31 Aug., 1688.

Paper, folio.   pp. 35 + a few blank.   Marbled boards ; gilt edges.

The signatures of the Commissioners are original, and possibly the Report itself.   **[2824.]**

[*Cf.* Pepys's *Memoirs of the Royal Navy*, and MSS. Nos. 1490, 1534 and 2823 *supra*].

The Voyage of William Ambrosia Cowley, mariner . . . .

Paper, folio.   pp. 110, paged as 285-394 + 4 pp. blank.   Marbled boards ; leather back.

"From the Capes of Virginia to the Islands of Cape D' Verd ; from thence to Guinea, and so to 60 degrees and 20 minutes South Latitude, round about Terra Del Fuego ; thence to the Northward in the South Sea as low as Panama ; from thence to the Island of Gorgonia, and so to the Ladroones; thence to China, so to Java, then to the Cape of Good Hope, and so to Holland; performed by him in several ships successively between 4 Aug., 1683, and 1 Oct., 1686."

[2826.]

[*See* Captain Cowley's Voyage round the Globe, printed in Hacke's *Voyages*, Lond., 1699.]

Rules, Orders, and Instructions for the future Government of the Office of the Ordnance.

Paper, folio.   pp. 108 unpaged.   Dark blue morocco, with elaborate gilt-tooled panel ; gilt edges.

Contents.   A statement of the duties of officers of the Ordnance, with an establishment of annual payments and allowances—as confirmed 25 July, 1683; with additions and amendments of 4 Feb., 1686–7. Followed by "a general list of the officers (superior and inferior) serving his Majesty in the Office of the Ordnance at the time of his signing the last preceding establishment."   **[2827.]**

[This manuscript is discussed in *Catalogue of Pepysian MSS.* i. 242-4.]

Transcript of the Index to the Trevor Papers.

Paper, folio.   pp. 126 unpaged, a few blank.   Standard binding.

Contents.   "A Transcript of Arthur Trevor's general alphabet to his MSS. common-place books lent me by Sir John Trevor, in order to my knowing whither to resort for anything contained therein and not

comprised within my collection of extracts out of the same under the title of Trevoriana, No. 1350—with copies of two lesser alphabets of his."
[2829.]
[The old shelf-mark No. 1350 was afterwards altered by Pepys, and is now No. 2217 *q.v. supra.*]

Sir William Monson's Six books of Discourses touching the Navy, in two volumes.

Paper, folio. Vol. I (books i. and ii.), pp. 476 ; + vol. II (books iii, iv., v. and vi.), pp. 413 + 16 pp. table of contents unpaged. Standard binding. [2834.]
[Sir William Monson's Discourses are in course of publication by the Navy Records Society, under the editorship of Mr. Oppenheim. See *Publications*, vols. xxii. and xxiii ; the principal manuscripts are referred to in the Introduction.]

Mr. Holland's Second Discourse touching the Navy. Written about the year 1659 . . . .

Paper, folio. pp. 213 + dedication and some blank pages. Standard binding. [2835.]
[See note to MS. No. 2193 *supra*. The extant manuscripts of this "Discourse" are described in *N.R.S.* Publications, vol. vii. pp. lxix–lxx. The author's signature elsewhere is clearly "John Hollond," and the signature to the Dedication of this MS. appears to have been altered from "Hollond" to "Holland" by an erasure.]

A General Alphabeto-Classico-Chronological Index of Matters Marine and Naval contained in my Transcript of the Parliament Rolls.

Paper, folio. pp. 299 (and some missing) + 16 pp. ruled off for further entries. Very dilapidated boards. [2846.]
[The transcript referred to is in MSS. Nos. 2840-2845.]

Admiralty Letters. 14 vols. marked as Vols. II—XV.

Paper, folio. Vols. ii—ix, vellum, with gilt tooling and red label ("S.P.'s Letters, Admiralty ") ; vols. x—xv, rough calf, with similar label.

Contents. These fourteen volumes constitute the letter-book of Pepys's office, during his tenure of the Secretaryship of the Admiralty, and are the seventeenth-century equivalent of a modern letter-copying book. The period covered by the correspondence is as follows :—

Vol. II [No. 2849. Ledger index 92 pages, 455 written pages, numbered as 453 pages + a few blank], 19 June, 1673, to 31 December,

1673. Vol. III [No. 2850. Ledger index 62 pages, 428 written pages], 1 January, 1673-4, to 31 December, 1674. Vol. IV [No. 2851. Ledger index 54 pages, 397 written pages + some blank], 1 January, 1674-5, to 10 April, 1676. Vol. V. [No. 2852. Ledger index 59 pages, 404 written pages + a few blank], 10 April, 1676, to 7 May, 1677. Vol. VI [No. 2853. Ledger index 62 pages, 483 written pages + a few blank], 7 May, 1677, to 25 March, 1678. Vol. VII [No. 2854. Ledger index 58 pages, 416 written pages], 25 March, 1678, to 1 August, 1678. Vol. VIII [No. 2855. Ledger index 62 pages, 473 written pages], 1 August, 1678, to 31 December, 1678. Vol. IX [No. 2856. No index. 284 written pages + 248 blank unpaged], 1 January, 1678-9, to 21 May, 1679. Vol. X [No. 2857. Ledger index 74 pages, 492 written pages], 23 May, 1684, to 20 May, 1685. Vol. XI [No. 2858. Ledger index 80 pages, 575 written pages + a few blank], 20 May, 1685, to 14 February, 1685-6. Vol. XII [No. 2859. Ledger index 102 pages, 491 written pages + a few blank], 15 February, 1685-6, to 8 March, 1686-7. Vol. XIII [No. 2860. Ledger index 84 pages, 452 written pages], 8 March, 1686-7, to 19 December, 1687. Vol. XIV [No. 2861. Ledger index 94 pages, 422 written pages], 1 January, 1687-8, to 13 September, 1688. Vol. XV [No. 2862. Ledger index 114 pages, 598 written pages + a few blank], 15 September, 1688, to 5 March, 1688-9.   [2849 to 2862.]

[These volumes are described in the introductions to vols. ii and iii of the *Catalogue of Naval MSS. in the Pepysian Library* (*N.R.S.* Publications, vols. xxvii and xxxvi), where the whole of the first four volumes of letters (vols. ii–v) have been printed in abstract. It is proposed to complete these abstracts in subsequent volumes of the series. A few of them have been catalogued in B.M. Add. MSS. No. 30220, by an earlier hand. There is reason to believe that vol. i of "S.P.'s Letters" was missing from the Library when it came into John Jackson's hands at Pepys's death in 1704. The entry in Jackson's *Additamenta* to Pepys's *Supellex Literaria* is left blank as to title and date of contents, but there is an earlier shelf-mark indicated.]

Admiralty Journal. 1 Jan., 1673-4, to 21 April, 1679.

Paper, folio. pp. 4 blank + pp. 1144, all unpaged. Marbled boards; leather back.

Contents. Minutes of the Commission of the Admiralty, from the date when the orders and warrants of the Commissioners ceased to be entered among "Admiralty Letters" [See MS. No. 2849] until the dissolution of the Commission.   [2865.]

[Vol. ii of the *Admiralty Letters* (to 31 December, 1673) contains these orders and warrants, but subsequent volumes do not].

Naval Minutes.

Paper, folio. pp. 460, but pp. 388-460 are blank. Marbled boards with leather back; much worn.

Contents. Miscellaneous memoranda, some of them probably notes for Pepys's projected History of the Navy. They include (p. 305) a copy of "Mr. Hewer's account of the Secretaries of the Admiralty from 1660 to 1688." Inserted opposite p. 1 are 14 pp. small folio containing "An Extract of Papers in Chartophyl. Regio relating to our Admiralty and Navy Affairs"—a list of the titles of various papers, with their dates. Inserted opposite p. 386 are 4 pp. small folio: "1654, Captain Fowler's Discourse with a Dutch Skipper how the English came to beat the Dutch at Sea; given me by Mr. Gibson."

[2866.]

[Some extracts from this MS. are printed in Derrick, *Memoirs of the Royal Navy*, pp. 46n, 84, 85, 89n, 98, and in *Catalogue of Pepysian MS.* i, 5, 40n, 50n, 60, 61, 64-5, 91, 127, 151, 166n, 178n, 225-8, 233n, 245-7].

Navy and Admiralty Precedents.

Paper, folio. pp. 668 + many blank; pp. 12, table of contents. Marbled boards; leather back. **[2867]**

Contents. "A collection of naval forms and other papers serving for information and precedents in most of the principal occasions of the Admiralty and Navy calling for the same." An index to the volume is in B.M. Add. MSS. 30221. The following is a complete list of the documents contained in it:

P. 1.—[1 Jan., 1686–7.] A general list of the ships of the royal navy.
[*Cf.* MS. No. 2940.]

P. 13.—[1 Jan., 1686–7.] A general list of the names of persons this day in employment in the admiralty and royal navy.
[*Cf.* MS. No. 2762 and 2941.]

P. 35.—13 June, 1673. Order of council establishing the Lord High Admiral's instructions.
[See *Catalogue of Pepysian MSS.* i. 36. Other copies of the instructions are in MS. No. 2870 (*Miscellanies* ii. 401), in MS. No. 2902 (*Day Collection,* p. 10) and in S.P. Dom. Car. II, 335, No. 303; see also below, p. 149.]

P. 39.—10 June, 1684. Patent erecting an office of secretary for the affairs of the admiralty of England and appointing Mr. Pepys thereto.
[See *Catalogue of Pepysian MSS.* i. 65. Other copies are in MS. No. 2902 (*Day Collection,* p. 1), and in *Admiralty Letters,* x. 1. The original patent was bought by the College 50 or 60 years ago and is preserved in the Pepysian Library.]

P. 40.—13 Jan., 1682[–3]. Patent constituting Henry, Duke of Grafton, vice-admiral of England.

[See *Catalogue of Pepysian MSS.* i. 65. *Cf.* MS. No. 2874 (*Miscellanies* vi. 171).]

P. 42.—20 Feb., 1684[–5]. Patent constituting Arthur Herbert, Esq., rear-admiral of England.

[Extract in *Catalogue of Pepysian MSS.* i. 65; *cf.* also MS. No. 2874 (*Miscellanies* vi. 175, 177).]

P. 48.—10 Dec., 1683. Patent constituting Sir Richard Haddock, Knight, Anthony Sturt, John Parsons, and Nicholas Fenn, Esqs., commissioners for victualling his Majesty's navy, with instructions to them for the well-management thereof.

[Discussed in *Catalogue of Pepysian MSS.* i. 180.]

P. 64.—13 Mar., 1685–6. Warrant to the attorney-general to prepare a bill constituting Sir John Tippetts, Sir Richard Haddock, and Mr. Sotherne commissioners for adjusting the accounts of the navy to 25 March, 1686; and Sir Anthony Deane, Sir John Narbrough, Sir John Berry, Sir John Godwin, and Mr. Hewer, commissioners for the growing service thereof from that time.

[See below, p. 84. Another copy is in MS. No. 1490, p. 155; see also *Catalogue of Pepysian MSS.* i. 80, 85.]

P. 69.—13 Mar., 1685–6. Warrant to the attorney-general to prepare a bill constituting Sir Phineas Pett commissioner of his Majesty's navy for Chatham and Sheerness yards.

[See below, p. 111; see also *Catalogue of Pepysian MSS.* i. 83. Another copy is in MS. No. 1490, p. 167.]

P. 73.—13 Mar., 1685–6. The same for Sir Richard Beach at Portsmouth.

[See below, p. 131; see also *Catalogue of Pepysian MSS.* i. 85. Another copy is in MS. No. 1490, p. 175.]

P. 76.—13 Mar., 1685–6. The same for Balthazar St. Michel, Esq., for Deptford and Woolwich yards.

[See below, p. 121; see also *Catalogue of Pepysian MSS.* i. 85. Another copy is in MS. No. 1490, p. 183.]

P. 80.—17 Mar., 1685–6. Warrant to the attorney-general to provide a clause in each of the commissioners of the navy's patents for allowing them £500 per annum.

[Another copy is in MS. No. 1490, p. 195.]

P. 81.—23 Mar., 1685–6. Warrant empowering Sir John Tippetts, Sir Richard Haddock, Sir Anthony Deane, Sir John Narbrough, Sir John Berry, Sir John Godwin, and Sir Phineas Pett, Knights, James Sotherne and William Hewer, Esqs., (together with the treasurer of the navy), to assemble together and proceed to the adjustment of all things which shall require the same, before the passing of their respective patents.

[Noted in *Catalogue of Pepysian MSS.* i. 85. Another copy is in MS. 1490, pp. 203–5.]

P. 83.—25 March, 1686. Warrant empowering the same persons to proceed to the execution of the charge and duty of commissioners of the navy till the passing of their patents.

[Noted in *Catalogue of Pepysian MSS.* i. 85. Another copy is in MS. 1490, pp. 207–9.]

P. 84.—17 April, 1686. Patent constituting Sir Anthony Deane, Sir John Narbrough, Sir John Berry, Sir John Godwin, and Mr. Hewer commissioners for managing the affairs of the navy from the 25th of March, 1686, and Sir John Tippetts, Sir Richard Haddock, and Mr. Sotherne for the adjusting all accounts depending at that day, with instructions to each of them in the execution thereof.

[Summarised in *Catalogue of Pepysian MSS.* i. 80. See above, p. 64; another copy is in MS. 1490, p. 261.]

P. 111.—19 April, 1686. Patent constituting Sir Phineas Pett commissioner of his Majesty's navy for Chatham and Sheerness yards, with instructions to him for his government in the execution of his duty therein.

[Summarised in *Catalogue of Pepysian MSS.* i. 83. See also above, p. 69.]

P. 121.—19 April, 1686. The same for Balthazar St. Michel, Esq., for Deptford and Woolwich yards.

[Noted in *Catalogue of Pepysian MSS.* i. 85. Another copy is in MS. 1490, p. 323; see also above, p. 76.]

P. 131.—19 April, 1686. The same for Sir Richard Beach, Knight, for Portsmouth yard.

[Noted in *Catalogue of Pepysian MSS.* i. 85. See above, p. 73; *cf.* also MS. 1490, p. 347.]

P. 141.—28 July, 1660. Warrant to the judge of the admiralty to prepare letters patents constituting the Earl of Sandwich vice-admiral of his Majesty's navy and admiral of the narrow seas.

[*Cf.* MS. No. 2871 (*Miscellanies* iii. 599, 602, 606).]

P. 142.—16 July, 1672. Commission appointing his Highness Prince Rupert vice-admiral of England.

P. 144.—[9] July, 1673. Patent constituting Prince Rupert, Earl of Shaftesbury, Lord Viscount Osborne, Earl of Anglesey, Duke of Buckingham, Duke of Monmouth, Duke of Lauderdale, Duke of Ormonde, Earl of Arlington, Sir George Carteret, Henry Coventry, and Edward Seymour, Esqrs., commissioners for executing the office of Lord High Admiral of England.

[This copy is dated 19 July in error, but see *Catalogue of Pepysian MSS.* i. 38*n*; other copies, correctly dated 9 July, are in MS. 2902 (*Day Collection,* p. 46), and MS. No. 2870 (*Miscellanies* ii. 405).]

P. 149.—13 June, 1673. Order of council establishing the Lord High Admiral's instructions [see above, p. 35].

P. 153.—[30 April, 1663.] The duty of a judge-advocate of the fleet enquired into and ascertained.

P. 156.—[13 April, 1686]. An establishment about volunteers and midshipmen extraordinary.

[Discussed in *Catalogue of Pepysian MSS.* i. 214. *Cf.* MS. No. 2902 (*Day Collection,* p. 13).]

P. 161.—[15 December, 1677.] Resolutions taken by his Majesty for the better regulating the choice of chaplains for the future service of his ships at sea.

[Discussed in *Catalogue of Pepysian MSS.* i. 206. Another copy is in MS. 2902 (*Day Collection*, p. 19).]

P. 163.—[13 March, 1686-7.] An alteration therein touching the signers of the certificates required on that behalf.

[See *Catalogue of Pepysian MSS.* i. 206.]

P. 164.—6 May, 1674. Order of council establishing an allowance of half-pay to captains of 1st and 2nd rate ships and 2nd captains of flagships.

[Summarised in *Catalogue of Pepysian MSS.* i. 146. Another copy is in MS. 2902 (*Day Collection*, p. 25). See also below, p. 259.]

P. 165.—19 May, 1675. Order of council establishing an allowance of half-pay to such commanders as shall have the command of 12 ships of war, besides fireships and small craft.

[Summarised in *Catalogue of Pepysian MSS.* i. 147. Another copy is in MS. No. 2902 (*Day Collection*, p. 28).]

P. 167.—19 May, 1675. Order of council establishing an allowance [of half-pay] to masters of 1st and 2nd rate ships.

[Summarised in *Catalogue of Pepysian MSS.* i. 147. See also below, p. 261. Another copy is in MS. No. 2902 (*Day Collection*, p. 29).]

P. 169.—19 May, 1684. Patent revoking the commission of the admiralty.

[See *Catalogue of Pepysian MSS.* i. 65. Another copy is in MS. No. 2902 (*Day Collection*, p. 54).]

P. 170.—25 October, 1685. Commission appointing Jonathan Gauden, Esq., agent-general and muster-master at Gibraltar, with instructions for his well discharging his duty therein.

P. 174.—29 Dec., 1679. Commissioners of the admiralty's letter of retrenchment of the King's charge in the navy.

[Discussed in *Catalogue of Pepysian MSS.* i. 62. Another copy is in MS. No. 2902 (*Day Collection*, p. 55).]

P. 179.—The duties of the vice-admirals of England and their sub-officers.

P. 182.—11 March, 1686-7. Lord Sunderland's letter to Sir Martin Wescombe, consul at Cadiz, accompanying a process against Thomas Daniel, master of a merchant ship called the Jerusalem [with the said process annexed].

P. 186.—The ancient custom in Queen Elizabeth's time concerning the several shares and other duties that doth any way appertain to the officers of men-of-war upon occasion of prizes.

[Printed in *Catalogue of Pepysian MSS.* i. 212*n*.]

P. 189.—Representation of the merchants about their being supplied with convoys upon the score of a war with Algiers [1676?].

[A note on this document is in *Catalogue of Pepysian MSS.* iii, p. xvi*n*.]

P. 192.—An account of the ships annually employed on the herring, Turkey, Newfoundland, Iceland, Italian, and Canary convoys in and since the year 1680.

P. 195.—10 Feb., 1685-6. A table of monthly wages allowed to the several officers and seamen in his Majesty's ships, by which they have formerly been paid; and since the time of Sir Richard Haddock, Knight, present comptroller of the navy, 1685-6.

P. 196.—15 Feb., 1685-6. A table of the monthly wages humbly proposed by the principal officers and commissioners of his Majesty's navy as fitting to be established for the officers and others serving on board his Majesty's ships.
[Printed in *Catalogue of Pepysian MSS.* i. 150.]

P. 197.—Table for the calculation of wages.

P. 198.—6 Dec., 1672. Order of council establishing allowances to superannuated officers in the navy.
[Summarised in *Catalogue of Pepysian MSS.* i. 148. Another copy is in MS. No. 2902 (*Day Collection*, p. 65).]

P. 199.—16 Aug., 1687. An account of the present force of Algiers by sea.
[*Cf.* MS. No. 2873 (*Miscellanies* v. 239); MS. No. 2874 (*ib.* vi. 267); MS. No. 2875 (*ib.* vii. 497); MS. No. 2879 (*ib.* xi. 97).]

P. 201.—22 Dec., 1677. Lords commissioners of the admiralty's letter to the master of the ordnance accompanying an establishment of guns for the royal navy, with the establishment itself.
[Discussed and summaries printed in *Catalogue of Pepysian MSS.* i. 233-7. *Cf.* also MS. No. 1340 and MS. No. 2902 (*Day Collection*, p. 59). The establishment had been confirmed by the King and lords of the admiralty, 3 Nov., 1677.]

P. 211.—Form of the letters given to persons for their examinations as to lieutenants [1687].
[See p. 241 below.]

P. 212.—2 Nov., 1687. The present disposal of all his Majesty's ships in sea pay.

P. 214.—A table of the going out and the coming in of the foreign posts.

P. 215.—[17 April, 1686]. A solemn conference with the master builders of England touching the use of east country plank in the royal navy.
[See *Catalogue of Pepysian MSS.* i. 64, and Pepys's *Memoirs of the Royal Navy;* also MS. No. 2879 (*Miscellanies*, xi, 1).]

P. 217.—26 Feb., 1665[-6]. Order of council establishing allowances to vice and rear-admirals of a fleet and squadron.
[Noted in *Catalogue of Pepysian MSS.* i. 140. *Cf.* also MS. No. 2902 (*Day Collection*, p. 21).]

P. 218.—[6 June, 1673]. Order of council establishing rewards to officers wounded in service at sea.
[Summarised in *Catalogue of Pepysian MSS.* i. 148. Other copies are in MS. No. 2874 (*Miscellanies*, vi. 67) and in MS. No. 2902 (*Day Collection*, p. 23).]

P. 219.—[15 Oct., 1673]. Order of council establishing rewards to volunteers and land-officers wounded at sea.
[Summarised in *Catalogue of Pepysian MSS.* i. 149. *Cf.* also MS. 2902 (*Day Collection*, p. 83).]

P. 220.—[6 Feb., 1673-4]. Order of council establishing rewards to officers who have received wounds at sea equal to the loss of an eye or limb.
[Summarised in *Catalogue of Pepysian MSS.* i. 149.]

P. 221.—[27 Mar., 1674]. Order of council establishing a reward to flag-officers wounded at sea.
[Noted in *Catalogue of Pepysian MSS.* i. 149*n*. Other copies are in MS. No. 2902 (*Day Collection*, p. 24), and MS. No. 2874 (*Miscellanies*, vi. 69).]

P. 222.—[26 June, 1674]. Order of council establishing allowances to vice and rear-admirals of fleets and squadrons and captains of admiral ships.
[Noted in *Catalogue of Pepysian MSS.* i. 145. Another copy is in MS. 2902 (*Day Collection*, p. 27).]

P. 224.—[10 July, 1679]. Order of council directing what style shall be used by the commissioners of the admiralty in their letters to the master of the ordnance, and requiring him to obey their warrants in matters relating to the navy. [The style is "pray and desire."]

P. 225.—[20 Oct., 1685]. Instructions for the execution of the duty required from the guard-ships and boats in Chatham and Portsmouth harbours.
[An account of this document is given in *Catalogue of Pepysian MSS.* i. 208.]

P. 236.—14 May, 1679. Patent constituting Sir Henry Capel, Daniel Finch, Esq., Sir Thomas Lee, Sir Humphrey Winch, Sir Thomas Meres, Edward Vaughan, and Edward Hales, Esqrs., commissioners for the affairs of the admiralty of England.
[Noted in *Catalogue of Pepysian MSS.* i. 57. Other copies are in MS. No. 2902 (*Day Collection*, p. 50), and MS. No. 2870 (*Miscellanies* ii. 413).]

P. 241.—22 Dec., 1677. Lords commissioners of the admiralty's letter to the navy board accompanying the rules established for ascertaining the duty of a sea-lieutenant, and for examining persons pretending to that office.
[Discussed in *Catalogue of Pepysian MSS.* i. 203. An extract from this document is in MS. No. 2902 (*Day Collection*, p. 17). See also p. 211 above.]

P. 245.—15 July, 1686. Establishment about plate-carriage and allowance for captains' tables, with an order of exception to that part of it which relates to the business of passengers [dated 22 October, 1686].
[Discussed in *Catalogue of Pepysian MSS.* i. 210. Another copy is in MS. No. 2902 (*Day Collection*, p. 84), and the establishment is printed in Pepys's *Memoirs relating to the State of the Royal Navy*, pp. 102-126.]

P. 253-9.—Forms of commission and warrant to naval officers. [C.R. and J.R.]

P. 259.—Order of the lords of the admiralty for allowing half-pay to commanders of 1st and 2nd rate ships.
[In pursuance of the order of council of 6 May, 1674, on p. 164 above. "1684" is written for 1674 in the text.]

P. 261.—Orders of the lords of the admiralty for allowing half-pay to masters of 1st and 2nd rate ships.
[In pursuance of the order of council of 19 May, 1675, on p. 167 above. Here also "1684" is written in error for 1674. The copy was probably made in the book in or about 1685, so the mistake was natural.]

P. 262.—[Form of] warrant for establishing a pension upon officers superannuated in the service.

P. 263.—4 July, 1685. Warrant appointing Charles Porter, Esq., counsel for the navy.

P. 265.—[15 Dec., 1686.] Warrant appointing James Pearse, Esq., chyrurgeon-general of the navy.

P. 265.—17 Dec., 1686. Warrant appointing Sir Richard Raines, Kt., judge of the admiralty.

P. 266.—13 Sept., 1685. Commission appointing Dr. Thomas Pinfold advocate-general for the office of high admiral of England.

P. 268.—9 Mar., 1684–5. Warrant granting Mr. Bedford the reversion of the place of principal register of the high court of admiralty.
[*Cf.* MS. No. 2874 (*Miscellanies* vi. 187).]

P. 269.—5 Mar., 1684–5. Warrant continuing Mr. Joynes as marshal of the admiralty.
[*Cf.* MS. No. 2874 (*Miscellanies* vi. 183).]

P. 270.—[24 Feb., 1684–5.] Warrant continuing Sir Robert Holmes, Knight, as vice-admiral of the county of Hampshire and the Isle of Wight.

P. 270.—[24 June, 1685.] Warrant continuing Dr. Watkinson as judge of the vice-admiralty of Hampshire and the Isle of Wight.

P. 271.—[23 July, 1673.] Commission appointing Samuel Franklin procurator in all causes, ecclesiastical and marine.

P. 274.—19 May, 1683. Lords commissioners of the admiralty their commission to Robert Yard, Esq. to be muster-master in the narrow seas, with instructions annexed for his better executing the said office.

P. 277.—5 June, 1679. Instructions to Captain Laurence Wright, commander-in-chief of the convoy to the Newfoundland Fishery, with heads of enquiries to be made by him upon his arrival there.
[See *Catalogue of Pepysian MSS.* vol. iii, p. xxiv*n.*]

P. 284.—17 May, 1681. Instructions to Captain Killigrew, commander-in-chief of the convoy to the ships trading into Spain, Italy, and the Mediterranean.

P. 286.—4 Oct., 1681. Instructions to Captain Allen, commander-in-chief of the convoy to the ships trading to the Canaries.

P. 287.—22 Jan., 1682–3. Instructions to Captain Hamilton, commander-in-chief of the convoy to the ships trading into the Mediterranean.

P. 289.—[17 Jan., 1682–3.] Order of council about passes [and various papers relating thereto].
[The question of passes in relation to the years 1675-82 is discussed in *Catalogue of Pepysian MSS.* vol. iii. pp. xviii-xxiv.]

P. 310.—1 Jan., 1683–4. Lord Dartmouth's instructions to the commanders of each of his Majesty's ships under his command at Tangier.

P. 313.—7 October, 1680. Instructions to Captain Trevanion, commander-in-chief of the ships appointed to guard the herring fishery at Yarmouth.

P. 314.—12 May, 1681. Instructions to Captain Tyrrell, appointed convoy to ships bound to Iceland.

P. 315.—6 December, 1681. Instructions to Captain Carverth, commander-in-chief of the convoy appointed to the ships bound with herrings, etc., into the Mediterranean.

P. 317.—3 August, 1684. Instructions to Captain Killigrew, commander of the Mordaunt, lent by his Majesty to the Royal African Company for a voyage to Guinea.

P. 320.—23 October, 1684. Instructions to Captain Tyrrell, commander of the Phoenix, employed in the service of the East India Company in a voyage to the East Indies.

P. 325.—2 Feb., 1685–6. Instructions to Captain Talbot, commander of the Falcon, appointed to attend on the Island of Jamaica.

P. 335.—[17 January, 1672–3.] Order of council directing a commission to be prepared appointing several persons therein named to be commissioners for distributing relief to the widows and orphans of persons slain at sea in the Dutch War [with the said commission and instructions for the commissioners annexed].

[Briefly summarised in *Catalogue of Pepysian MSS.* i. 134. *Cf.* also MS. 2874 (*Miscellanies* vi. 47). A copy of part of the document is in MS. No. 2902 (*Day Collection,* p. 67).]

P. 342.—21 December, 1674. Order to the navy board referring to them the execution of the aforesaid commission upon the vacancy thereof, and to distribute the King's bounty to the relations of persons slain at sea. [This is extended by a letter from the lords of the admiralty, dated 25 September, 1678, to service against Algiers, and by another dated 10 January, 1681-2, to service against the Moors at Tangier.]

[Noted in *Catalogue of Pepysian MSS.* i. 134. See also p. 481 below.]

P. 344.—[31 October, 1686.] Instructions to . . . Captain Henry Killigrew, commander of . . . the Dragon, and commander-in-chief . . . in the present war with Sallee.

P. 350.—[4 July, 1660.] Order of council empowering his Royal Highness to appoint Sir George Carteret treasurer, and the Lord Berkeley, Sir William Penn, and Peter Pett, Esq., commissioners of the navy, to join with and assist the comptroller, surveyor, and clerk of the acts thereof.

[See *Catalogue of Pepysian MSS.* i. 7, where the date is given in error as 2 July. Other copies are in MS. No. 2611 (Penn's *Naval Collections,* p. 113) and Bodl. Rawlinson MSS. A. 466, f. 10.]

P. 352.—[28 January, 1661-2.] His Royal Highness's letter to the navy board directing their inspecting into and reforming several abuses crept into the navy, and enjoining the execution of instructions framed for their general direction in the economy of the royal navy.

[See *Catalogue of Pepysian MSS.* i. 21. Another copy is in MS. No. 2611 (Penn's *Naval Collections,* p. 121). Printed in Penn, *Memorials of Sir William Penn* ii. 265.]

P. 356.— [28 January, 1661-2]. Warrant accompanying his book of the general instructions of principal officers and commissioners of the navy and under-officers thereof. [The instructions follow.]

[Discussed in *Catalogue of Pepysian MSS.* i. 20-1. Another copy is in MS. No. 2611 (Penn's *Naval Collections,* p. 127); and the first part of the instructions is copied into MS. No. 2242, pp. 1-18. They were printed in 1717 from an imperfect copy under the title *The Œconomy of H.M.'s Navy Office* (*D.N.B.* xxix, 183). See also Bodl. Rawlinson MSS. A. 466.]

P. 399.—18 July, 1662. His Royal Highness's letter to the navy officers about their taking security from the several pursers of his Majesty's ships for the well performance of their duty.

[Noted in *Catalogue of Pepysian MSS.* i. 23.]

P. 401.—[15 March, 1669-70.] The Duke of York's order allowing the commissioners of the outports to act for the King's service without orders from the body of the board, in cases where they cannot wait for the same without inconvenience to the service.

[Noted in *Catalogue of Pepysian MSS.* i. 19, where the date is given in error as 1668-9.]

P. 402.—The ordinary estimate of the annual charge of the royal navy for the year 1684.

[This document is discussed in *Catalogue of Pepysian MSS.* i. 111-115.]

P. 416.—31 December, 1677. The contract for victualling the royal navy.
[This document is fully discussed in *Catalogue of Pepysian MSS*. i. 165-177.]

P. 455.—31 December, 1674. Contract between the King and Sir Thomas Clutterbuck for victualling his Majesty's ships in the Mediterranean.
[Noted in *Catalogue of Pepysian MSS*. i. 165.]

P. 473.—19 February, 1676[-7]. A supplemental contract between the King and Sir Thomas Clutterbuck, relating to some alterations to be made in that of 31 December, 1674 [above, p. 455], for victualling his Majesty's ships in the Mediterranean.
[Noted in *Catalogue of Pepysian MSS*. i. 165*n*.]

P. 475.—A table shewing the victuallers' gain and his Majesty's loss arising from the price paid them by him for each species of sea-provisions delivered in broken proportions, with the pursers' concernments therein.
[On " broken proportions " see *Catalogue of Pepysian MSS*. i. 174.]

P. 476.—20 Jan., 1667[-8]. An order made by the King in council for paying to the Poor's Chest at Chatham all moneys stopped out of seamen's wages for neglect of duty, and the groats allowed to the minister in ships where there happens to be none.

P. 477.—17 July, 1668. An order made by the King in council establishing pensions to flag-officers during their being out of employment.
[Summarised in *Catalogue of Pepysian MSS*. i. 145. Another copy is in MS. No. 2902 (*Day Collection*, p. 22).]

P. 478.—30 July, 1673. An order made by the King in council forbidding the commanders of the King's ships to take any more than one per cent. for moneys carried from place to place belonging to the King's subjects.
[Noted in *Catalogue of Pepysian MSS*. i. 189.]

P. 479.—28 August, 1663. An order made in council exempting all the King's officers serving him in his navy and yards from bearing any office in their respective parishes.
[Discussed in *Catalogue of Pepysian MSS*. i. 144.]

P. 481.—10 February, 1687-8. His Majesty's order to the navy board accompanying and enjoining the execution of an order of council for allowing relief to the widows and orphans of persons slain in fight against any of his enemies at the seas [with the said order dated 3 February, 1687–8, annexed.]
[Noted in *Catalogue of Pepysian MSS*. i. 134. See also p. 342 above.]

P. 484.—26 August, 1668. His Royal Highness's letter to the commissioners of the navy reflecting upon several non-performances of the duties of their joint and particular offices—with respect to their instructions from the lord admiral.
[See *Catalogue of Pepysian MSS*. i. 28-30 and 30*n*. The first draft of this letter is in MS. No. 2242, pp. 25-47.]

P. 510.—25 November, 1668. His Royal Highness's letter to the navy board upon their answer to his letter of reflections [above, p. 484].
[See *Catalogue of Pepysian MSS*. i. 31-2 and 32*n*. The first draft of this letter and another copy of it in its final form are written out in parallel columns in MS. No. 2242, pp. 122-34.]

P. 519.—25 September, 1671.   His Royal Highness's letter to the navy board accompanying some additional and explanatory instructions for the better executing of the duty of the treasurer of the navy.
[Summarised in *Catalogue of Pepysian MSS.* i. 24.   Another copy is in Bodl. Rawlinson MSS. A. 466, f. 40*b*.]

P. 525.—30 July, 1673.   A clause in an order from the lords of the admiralty to the navy board directing them to prepare an establishment of cabins fit to be allowed to a ship of each rate in the royal navy [with the establishment proposed by them, 15 August, 1673, and the confirmation thereof by the lords of the admiralty, 16 October, 1673].
[The establishment is printed in *Catalogue of Pepysian MSS.* i. 189-92. *Cf.* also MS. No. 2902 (*Day Collection,* pp. 30-34).]

P. 530.—A table of rates adjusted by the master, wardens, and assistants of the Trinity House of Deptford Strond for the piloting of his Majesty's ships of every rank; with an assignment of the number of days to be allowed for the performance of each service mentioned therein.

P. 533.—8 Feb., 1672[-3].   Instructions to James Pearse, Esq., chyrurgeon-general of his Majesty's navy.
[See *Catalogue of Pepysian MSS.* i. 138.]

P. 534.—The number of clerks and servants allowed to the yard officers, carpenters of ships, and able workmen employed in the service of the navy.   [Establishment not dated.]

P. 536.—[8 March, 1671-2.]   Commissioners appointed to take care and provide for sick and wounded men at sea [with their instructions].
[They are also charged with the 'the relief of widows, children, and impotent parents of such as shall be slain in H.M.'s service at sea; as also for the ordering of prisoners of war.']
[Discussed in *Catalogue of Pepysian MSS.* i. 133.   Another copy is on pp. 613-18 below; *cf.* also MS. No. 2874 (*Miscellanies* vi. 47).]

P. 542.—[13 March, 1671-2.]   A general order for all officers to be assisting to the commissioners appointed for taking care of sick and wounded men at sea.   [Another copy is on pp. 618-19 below.]

P. 543.—[23 March, 1671-2.]   Instructions from the commissioners to their deputies for the taking care of sick and wounded seamen.
[Another copy is on pp. 619-21 below.]

P. 546.—[March, 1671-2.]   Instructions for a chyrurgeon appointed to take care of wounded seamen.
[Another copy is on pp. 622-3 below.]

P. 548.—[March, 1671-2.]   Instructions to a provost-marshal for taking care of all prisoners of war.
[See *Catalogue of Pepysian MSS.* i. 134.   Another copy is on pp. 623-4 below.]

P. 549.—[25 March, 1671-2.]   Appointment of Mr. John Bullock to be chief chyrurgeon at the port of Dover, with his instructions.
[Signed J. Evelyn.   Another copy is on pp. 624-5 below.]

P. 551.—[1673?] An abstract of certain instructions given the commissioners for the taking care of the sick and wounded men, and for the relief of widows, children, and impotent parents of such as shall be slain in his Majesty's service at sea.
[Another copy is on pp. 626-7 below.]

P. 553.—[26 November, 3 Jac. II.] The form of a commission of oyer and terminer for the admiralty. [*Latin.*]

P. 563.—[1 October, 1 Jac. II.] Form of a patent of a judge of the admiralty of England. [*Latin.*]

P. 570.—[6 September, 1660.] Form of a patent for the register of the admiralty of England. [*Latin.*]

P. 574.—[5 March, 1684–5]. Form of a warrant for the marshal of the high court of admiralty. [*Latin.*]

P. 575.—[4 July, 1686.] A warrant from his Majesty appointing William Oldys, Doctor of Laws, to be advocate-general for the office of high admiral of England.

P. 576.—[13 Feb., 1684–5.] His Majesty's warrant appointing Samuel Franckyn, Esq., procurator in all causes maritime and ecclesiastical.

P. 576.—[22 May, 1686.] Form of the patent for vice-admiral of a county in England. [*Latin.*]

P. 582.—[7 July, 1686.] Form of a patent for a judge of a vice-admiralty of a county in England. [*Latin.*]

P. 585.—[7 July, 1686.] Form of a patent for a register of a vice-admiralty of a county of England. [*Latin.*]

P. 586.—[7 July, 1686.] Form of a patent for a marshal of a vice-admiralty of a county of England. [*Latin.*]

P. 587.—[6 January, 1664–5.] A patent for constituting the principal commissioners for prizes during the present war with Holland [with instructions annexed].

P. 594.—A commission to the Lord High Admiral enabling him to grant letters of marque and reprisal [5 January, 1664-5] with instructions thereto annexed [28 January, 1664–5].

P. 598.—[4 February, 1664–5.] A commission of marque granted to Jacob Janson Governour, to set forth the ship Anne.

P. 600.—[16 December, 1664.] An order of council to the Lord High Admiral empowering him to grant general reprisals against the States of the United Provinces.

P. 601.—[22 February, 1664–5.] Rules and directions applied by his Majesty in council to be observed by the high court of admiralty in the adjudication of prizes.

P. 603.—[15 March, 1664–5.] An order from the Lord High Admiral forbidding the entertaining of more than four Englishmen in any ship fitted out with letters of marque.

P. 604.—31 July, [32 Car II]. Commission granted by his Majesty to the commissioners of the admiralty for issuing out commissions of reprisal against the people of Algiers.

P. 605.—An order from the admiralty for the granting a commission of reprisal to Robert Warner, master of the Four Brothers of London, against the people of Algiers [2 August, 1680] with the commission so granted annexed [1680].

[MS. "2 Aug., 1681," but it refers to the commission of "31 July last," and there is a reference on p. 606 to the warrant of 2 Aug., 1680.]

P. 610.—14 December, 1681. Instructions to such masters of merchant-ships who shall take out letters of marque against the government and people of Algiers.

P. 628.—[3 March, 1687-8.] Mr. James Pearse, chirurgeon-general, his account of the manner of appointing chirurgeons for his Majesty's ships, and the disposal of sick and wounded men.

P. 630.—Various forms relating to the appointment of chirurgeons and the care of sick and wounded men.

P. 634.—Form of masters of Trinity House's certificate for a master of any of his Majesty's ships.

P. 635.—The navy board's warrant for a master of one of his Majesty's ships.

P. 635.—The masters of Trinity House approbation of a pilot [168 . .].

P. 636.—Form of the masters of Trinity House licence to a waterman or wherryman to row in the River [168..].

P. 637.—[26 January, 1687-8?] Sir Richard Raines, judge of the admiralty, his opinion upon the two great points, whether desertion or a ship being paid off exempts offenders from trial, and of the number of captains to make up a court-martial.

P. 638.—[16 April, 1688.] An order to the navy board for paying all fines to the Chest at Chatham.

P. 638.—[30 March, 1688.] An order of council giving all fines, etc., to the Chest at Chatham.

P. 639.—[November, 1686.] The advice of the navy board touching an establishment for boatswains' and carpenters' sea stores [with the proposed establishment annexed].
   [Noted in *Catalogue of Pepysian MSS.* i. 216.]

A Miscellany of Matters Historical, Political, and Naval.

Paper, folio : 11 volumes.   Standard binding.   **[2869-79.]**

Volume I [2869]

[pp. 355 + pp. 2 table of contents, also copied by another hand to face p. 1.]

Besides copies of two papers relating to Prince Rupert's proceedings at Kinsale, Jan., 1648-9 [pp. 209, 213], and six miscellaneous papers from the Cottonian Library, *temp.* Henr. VII, Henr. VIII, and Elizabeth [pp. 319 [Vespasian C. xiv. f. 81], 329 [*ib.* f. 320], 335 [*ib.* f. 55], 343 [*ib.* f. 467], 347 (2) [*ib.* f. 444 and f. 79], the volume contains the following :—

P. 1.—King Henry VIII's first institution of and charter to the Trinity House of Deptford Strond [dated 20 March, 4 Hen. VIII], with the first acts and ordinances made therein.
   [Transcribed from the original entry in the Trinity House.]

P. 22.—Queen Elizabeth's charter to the said House . . . . [dated 11 Feb., 1 Eliz.]

P. 31.—A project for erecting a standing land militia in England, presented to King Philip, husband to Queen Mary, anno 1557.
[Another copy is in MS. 1774 *supra*.]

P. 51.—A journal of Phineas Pett, Esq., commissioner of the navy . . . . from his birth, anno 1570, to the arrival of the Royal Sovereign, by him then newly built, at her moorings at Chatham [1638]; transcribed from the original written all with his own hand, and lent me to that purpose by his grandson, Mr. Phineas, son to Captain Phineas Pett.
[Another journal of Phineas Pett, with variations and omissions, is in B.M. Harl. MSS. 6279. A great part of this MS. is printed, although probably from an imperfect transcript, in *Archaeologia*, xii, 217-296, and quotations from it are given in Derrick, *Memoirs of the Royal Navy*, pp. 40*n*, 47, 48, 49, 63*n*, 64-6, 67-8 : *c.f.* also Charnock, *Marine Architecture,* ii, 286-7. The Pepysian MS. is the better of the two.]

P. 187.—Arguments proving the King's Majesty's propriety in the sea lands and salt shores thereof . . . .

P. 215.—A scheme of a history of the plantations, proposed to Mr. Evelyn by one Mr. [William] London from the Barbados, 1680.

P. 221.—Sir John (then Captain Narbrough his journal on board the Prince, in which his Royal Highness went admiral against the Dutch . . . . from January 1671-2 to her coming-in September following.
[Transcribed 'from the original under Sir John Narbrough's own hand'. See MS. No. 2555 *supra*.]

P. 349.—A transcript of arguments asserting the King of England's sea dominion. [' B.M. Cott Vesp. cxiv.']

Volume II [2870]

[pp. 602 + pp. 12 table of contents.]

Copies of 137 miscellaneous documents, nearly all transcribed from Sir Julius Cæsar's Library. Those on pp. 1–88 are mainly financial papers of the early years of James I's reign, including, on p. 33, " Remarks upon the method, use, and imperfection of Exchequer tallies " [*temp*. Eliz.]. The rest are from Edward VI to Charles II, and include the following :

P. 97.—A remonstrance to the Lord Admiral from Trinity House of the decay of shipping and mariners in England, anno 1602.

P. 101.—The opinion of the Trinity House touching shares in time of war or reprisal, given by them anno 1594.

P. 113.—Rainsford's project for the prohibiting strangers to fish on the English coasts, anno 1604.
[On Richard Rainsford's 'project' of 1609, for which this can only be a preliminary sketch, see Fulton, *The Sovereignty of the Sea*, p. 138.]

P. 121.—Reasons touching the maintenance of English shipping, delivered to Sir Julius Cæsar, August 1609, by William Hollyday.

P. 125.—A petition from the Trinity House to King James, July 1609, touching the maintenance of English shipping, with motives to induce the King to grant their suit.
[*Cf*. B.M. Lansdowne MSS. cxlii. 43.]

P. 129.—A list of the King's ships and pinnaces, with their respective tonnages and men, anno 1603[-4].
  [Printed in Derrick, *Memoirs of the Royal Navy*, pp. 38-40.]

P. 131.—A catalogue of all the King's ships, with their respective tonnages, and charge of their victuals and men at sea for a day, a week, a month, and a year, December 1607.
  [Another copy is in MS. No. 2873 *infra* (*Miscellanies* v. 579). Printed in Derrick, *Memoirs of the Royal Navy*, pp. 41-3, but with the victualling charges omitted.]

P. 133.—A project for contracting the charge of his Majesty's navy . . . .
  [This is a copy of the first four pages of MS. No. 2735 *supra*, with some slight variations in the figures.]

P. 145.—A project written by Henry Martyn, gentleman, and dedicated to his Highness the Prince of Wales, touching a more perfect register of baptisings, marriages, and burials.

P. 161.—A petition from the Trinity House of Deptford to the Parliament touching the haven at Dover [*circ.* 1600].

P. 165-199.—Papers relating to the expense of the King's household [1610].

P. 291.—The names of all the prisoners in the Tower, 25 October, 1549.
  [*Cf.* B.M. Cott. MSS. Titus B ii, 67*, which is assigned with doubt to 1551.]

P. 301.—William Thomas's letter to the King [Edw. VI] accompanying a particular of several queries, moral and political.
  [*Cf.* B.M. Cott. MSS. Vesp. D xviii, ff. 1-45, and Titus B ii, f. 96; see also *The Works of William Thomas, clerk of the Privy Council in the year 1549*, London, 1774.]

P. 381.—A copy of Alcade Hamet's letter to Colonel Kirke, governor of Tangier [1682-3?].
  [See below, p. 581.]

P. 383.—A copy of the Emperor of Morocco's letter to the Governor of Tangier, 23 February 1682-3.
  [See below, p. 581.]

P. 389.—A commission to his Royal Highness, James Duke of York, constituting him Lord High Admiral of England, 29 January, 12 Charles II, 1660[-1].
  [*Latin.*]
  [Another copy is in MS. No. 2902 (*Day Collection*, p. 35).]

P. 401.—Instructions established by his Majesty in council for ascertaining the duty of the Lord High Admiral of England, 13 June 1673.
  [Described in *Catalogue of Pepysian MSS.* i. 36. Other copies are in MS. No. 2867 (*Naval Precedents*, pp. 35 and 149) and MS. No. 2902 (*Day Collection*, p. 10); and see also S.P. Dom. Car. II. 335, No. 303.]

P. 405.—A commission under the great seal constituting Prince Rupert and others commissioners for executing the office of Lord High Admiral of England, 9 July, 25 Charles II, 1673.
  [Noted in *Catalogue of Pepysian MSS.* i. 38. Other copies are in MS. No. 2867 (*Naval Precedents*, p. 144) and MS. No. 2902 (*Day Collection*, p. 46).]

P. 409.—The King's warrant to the attorney-general to prepare a bill containing a commission to Sir Henry Capel and others constituting them commissioners for executing the office of the Lord High Admiral of England, the same being generally (mutatis mutandis) transcribed from that to Prince Rupert, etc., now determined [1679].

P. 411.—A memorandum relating to the following commission.
[The substance of this is printed in *Catalogue of Pepysian MSS.* i. 57-8.]
P. 413.—A commission under the great seal constituting Sir Henry Capel and others commissioners for executing the office of Lord High Admiral of England, 14 May 1679.
[Discussed in *Catalogue of Pepysian MSS.* i. 58. Other copies are in MS. No. 2867 (*Naval Precedents*, p. 236), and MS. No. 2902 (*Day Collection*, p. 50).]
P. 453.—Mr. Pepys's heads for discourse in Parliament upon the business of the navy, anno 1676.
[This document is fully discussed in *Catalogue of Pepysian MSS.* i. 48-53, and 229-30. *Cf.* also MS. No. 2266 No. 119.]
P. 477.—Sir William Petty's scheme of naval philosophy.
[*Cf.* Sir William Petty's *Treatise of Naval Philosophy*, Dublin, 1691. A letter is printed in *The Life, Journals, and Correspondence of Samuel Pepys* i. 301, from Dr. Wood to Pepys, 'accompanying some papers containing Sir Willam Petty's scheme of naval philosophy.']
P. 489-503.—Papers relating to Sir William Petty's experiments about shipping [1683-4].
[*Cf.* MS. No. 2874 (*Miscellanies* vi. 1-30).]
P. 505.—A discourse made by Sir Robert Southwell before the Royal Society, 8 April 1675, touching water.
[Sir Robert Southwell, the diplomatist, was an intimate friend of Sir William Petty's, and on 1 December, 1690, he was elected President of the Royal Society, holding the office for five successive years (*D.N.B.* liii. 300-1).]
P. 541.—A bill for preservation and increase of timber, prepared by Mr. Freeman, with the joint care of the company of shipwrights, at the instance of Mr. Pepys, 1675.
[See *Catalogue of Pepysian MSS.* i. 50n.]
P. 581.—A copy of the Emperor of Morocco's letter to the King of England about the four years' peace agreed upon by his Majesty and him concerning Tangier [23 Feb., 1682-3].
[See above, p. 383.]

Volume III [2871]

[pp. 750 + pp. 12 table of contents.]

Copies of 101 miscellaneous papers, most of them *temp.* Eliz. and Jac. I.

P. 73.—An extract of a general catalogue of the officers of the crown in the time of Queen Elizabeth, with their fees [*circ.* 1587-91.] ['Ex chartophyl. Cæsariense.']
P. 117.—Intercursus Magnus, anni 1495[-6] [*Latin*]. ['Ex chartophyl. Cæsariense.']
P. 158.—Martial laws in the King's camp in the time of King Henry VI. ['Ex chartophyl. Cæsariense'].
[These follow closely the 'Ordinances of war made by King Henry V at Mawnt,' printed in Twiss, *The Black Book of the Admiralty*, i. 459-72.]

P. 177.—Ordinances and laws of the admiralty of England (in old French) in the time of Edward III and before. [' Ex chartophyl. Cæsariense '].
[Printed in Twiss, *The Black Book of the Admiralty*, i, 2-87.]

P. 206.—An inquisition (in old French) taken at Queenborough, 2 April, 1375, touching the ancient customs of the admiralty, etc.
[Printed in Twiss, *ib*. i. 132-177.]

P. 228.—The ordinance of King John at Hastings (in old French), anno 2 Reg. sui, about obliging foreigners to strike sail to his ships.
[Printed in Twiss, *ib*. i. 128-31, and fully discussed in the introduction.]

P. 233.—Lorrain's translation of the three foregoing documents.
[There is in the Pepysian Library a manuscript translation from Latin into French of *Mulieres non Homines*, by Paul Lorrain, dated 1 Jan., 1677-8 (No. 1234).]

P. 289.—A project of a form by an order of intrenchment for defence against a landing of any army how strong soever, supposed inexpugnable, being conveniently guarded, especially with some troops of horse, if the ground serve for it : directed to the Right Hon. the Lord Burghley, Lord High Treasurer of England. [' Ex chartophyl. Com. Ailesburgens.'].
[Another copy is MS. No. 2021 *supra*.]

P. 309.—The King's letters patents to the Earl of Kent constituting him Lord High Admiral of England, 30 July, 1461. [*Latin*]. [' Ex chartophyl. Com. Ailesburgens.']

P. 313.—The description of Milford Haven, with the roads, creeks, points, harbour, etc., within or near the same. [' Ex chartophyl. Com. Ailesburgens.']
[A better copy, with maps, is MS. No. 1296 *supra*.]

P. 355.—Regulations to be made in the navy in relation to several abuses crept into the same in these latter times, being the result of a general enquiry into the navy through all the parts thereof.
[Another copy by an earlier hand is MS. No. 2165 *supra*.]

P. 503.—A general discourse of the navy of England, containing orders and instructions to be established for the better government of the same.

P. 555.—A discourse concerning the cook-rooms in his Majesty's ships in the year 1618.

P. 563-580.—Papers relating to proposals for lessening the complements of men in the King's ships, 1619.

P. 581.—The report of the council of trade to the King concerning the trade and navigation of his Majesty's kingdom, 14 March, 1660[-1].

P. 586.—A supplemental proposal for the convoying merchants and promoting trade, grounded upon the foregoing advice of the council of trade.

P. 599.—His Royal Highness's commission to the Earl of Sandwich to be admiral in the narrow seas, 13 March, 1660[-1].
[*Cf*. MS. No. 2867 (*Naval Precedents*, p. 141), and pp. 602, 606 below.]

P. 602.—The King's grant to the Earl of Sandwich of the admiralship in the narrow seas for life, 1 April, 1661.
[*Cf*. pp. 599 above and 606 below.]

P. 606.—The Lord High Admiral's warrant to the Earl of Sandwich to be admiral of his Majesty's fleet for the then expedition, 10 May, 1661.
[*Cf*. pp. 599 and 602 above.]

P. 607.—The Lord High Admiral's warrant to Sir John Mennes to be captain of the Henry, and vice-admiral in the narrow seas, 18 May, 1661.

P. 609.—A letter concerning Sir Robert Mansell's demands of imprest money for preachers, chyrurgeons, etc., 2 Aug., 1620.

P. 610.—The officers of the navy's report concerning the accounts of Sir Robert Mansell relating to his layings-out for the fleet, 19 December, 1621.

P. 613.—A report touching the accounts of Sir Thomas Button relating to the navy, about the years 1618 and 1619.

P. 635.—A letter to the Lord Admiral concerning the settled allowances given to the Lord Admirals, vice-, and rear-admirals, captains, etc., 29 July, 1622.

P. 661.—A letter concerning a list of merchant-ships both in the river and at sea fit for his Majesty's service, from the Trinity House, 1665.

P. 669.—The number of merchant docks in the river of Thames, anno 1666, in whose hands they are, and ships of what rate they are capable of receiving.

P. 683.—A discourse upon the past and present state of his Majesty's navy, by Sir Robert Slingsby, late comptroller thereof, to his Royal Highness, anno 1660. ['From my Lord Dartmouth'].
[Another copy is in MS. No. 2193 *supra*.]

P. 699.—An estimate of the charge of fitting forth, keeping abroad, and discharging the five squadrons of ships therein mentioned, calculated for answering all the naval occasions of England. ['From my Lord Dartmouth'].

P. 712.—The general heads of things in the office of his Majesty's papers and records for business of state, to the year 1621. ['From my Lord Dartmouth'].

P. 723.—A project for commanders having the charge and management of the ship-victualling and not pursers; with a discourse touching the putting the victualling of the navy into contract or keeping it in the King's hands: about the year 1673. ['From my Lord Dartmouth'].
[This document is discussed in *Catalogue of Pepysian MSS.* i. 160.]

P. 736.—Remarks made by the Lord Dartmouth under his own hand upon the foregoing project . . . . ['From my Lord Dartmouth'].
[This document is discussed in *Catalogue of Pepysian MSS.* i. 164.]

P. 738.—Observations on the management of the surveyor-general of his Majesty's marine victualling his employment.
[Pepys himself was appointed surveyor-general of victualling in 1665: see *Catalogue of Pepysian MSS.* i. 154.]

P. 739.—A calculation of the profit arising upon the victualling of the navy by contract.
[It appears from a note in the margin that Pepys was invited to become a sharer in a proposed victualling contract, but declined.]

Volume IV [2872]

[pp. 793, including table of contents.]

This volume is a transcript of the Commonplace Book of Mr. Bedford, Register of the Admiralty, and the papers it contains relate almost

entirely to Admiralty affairs.   It contains copies of 117 documents;
these include :—

P. 1–10.—Tables of fees paid to the officials of the court of admiralty.

P. 11.—The whole series of the regular and ordinary proceedings of a suit in
the court of admiralty.

P. 12.—The charges attending the same.

P. 237.—An account of divers things concerning the King['s] dominion on the
British seas, right of the flag, and about firing and salutes.

P. 279.—Catalogus admiralorum Angliæ a tempore Henrici III, Anno Domini
1307 ad annum 1660. [*Latin.*]

P. 291.—An abstract of what hath for above a hundred years been granted to
the Lord Admiral by his patent. [*Latin.*]

P. 299.—A list of the advocates admitted in the admiralty since his Majesty's
happy restoration in 1660.

P. 463.—A list of the judges of the high court of the admiralty of England
from the fifth year of King Henry VIII to 16 February 1684–5.
[Another list is on p. 349.]

P. 471–490.—A collection of papers relating to the business of prizes.

P. 510.—Joshua Maisee, an engineer, his petition to the Duke for his Royal
Highness's grant to him of the wreck in the Sound of Mull [1683].
[The original is probably Bodl. Rawlinson MSS. A. 189, f. 422.]

P. 511—Archibald Miller's information [20 November, 1683] concerning the ship
called the Florence of Spain, sunk in Tippermory in the Sound of Mull.
["I saw one paper of Latin extracted out of the Spanish records that
there was 30 millions of cash on board the said ship " . . . Another copy
is in Bodl. Rawlinson MSS. A. 189, f. 423.]

P. 515.—An abstract of our Laws of Oleron and of the laws in the Black Book
of the Admiralty and of our maritime laws among the Acts of Parliament,
etc., comprised in an alphabetical table; with translations of the said
Laws of Oleron and those in the Black Book, by Mr. Bedford.
[This appears to be a transcript of a MS. originally in the Library of the
College of Advocates in Doctors Commons, but now in private hands, described in Twiss, *The Black Book of the Admiralty,* i. pp. xiv-xv; there
is another copy in the Library of All Souls' College, Oxford (Wynne
MSS. cclxvi). The dedication of the Pepysian MS. to Sir Leoline Jenkins
is dated 30 June, 1679. *Cf.* MS. No. 1266 *supra.*]

P. 759.—A transcript of the most ancient Sea Laws of England contained in the
Black Book of the Admiralty, from an old and elegant copy thereof in
vellum resting in the library of Sir Robert Cotton and lent me by my
honoured friend Sir John Cotton, 1694. [*Old French.*]
[Transcribed from B.M. Cott. MSS. Vespasian B xxii. The principal
MSS. of the Black Book are described in Twiss, *The Black Book of the
Admiralty,* i, pp. lxxvii-lxxxii, and the original French and an English
translation are printed on opposite pages, *ib.* pp. 2-177. *Cf.* also an inferior copy in MS. No. 2871 (*Miscellanies,* iii, 177).]

Volume V [2873]

[pp. 662 + pp. 9 table of contents and some blank.]

Copies of 83 miscellaneous documents, the greater part of which are *temp.* Car. II. These include:

P. 1.—A true discourse of the army which the King of Spain caused to be assembled in the haven of Lisbon . . . 1588 . . . . . translated out of French into English by Daniel Archdeacon.
[Printed London, 1588, and transcribed from the print. See Lowndes, *Bibliographer's Manual*, p. 2464.]

P. 49.—Sir Anthony Deane's observations relating to the state of his Majesty's fleet, anno 1674 [12 Oct.], presented to my Lord Treasurer Danby.
[Another copy is in Bodl. Rawlinson MSS. A. 175, f. 282. The substance of it is printed in *Catalogue of Pepysian MSS.* i. 43-5.]

P. 53–92.—Correspondence between Mr. Evelyn and Mr. Pepys in relation to naval matters [1680].
[Relating mainly to the navy of Edward III, the battle of Lepanto, and the antiquity of shipping.]

P. 93.—Monthly lists of the ships at sea, 6 Sept., and 2 Nov., 1675.

P. 101.—His Majesty's resolution concerning the going out and coming in of our merchants' fleet, 11 Dec., 1671.

P. 109.—The Duke of York's sailing instructions, 1672.

P. 121.—The Duke of York's fighting instructions, 1672.
[See Corbett, *Fighting Instructions,* p. 146 (*N.R.S.* Publications, vol. xxix).]

P. 133.—Instructions to be observed by all masters, pilots, ketches, hoys, and smacks attending the fleet [1672].

P. 137–176.—Relations of the battle with the Dutch, 28 May, 1672, by the Duke of York, the Comte d'Estrées, Captain John Narbrough, Captain Richard Haddock, Sir Edward Spragge, Sir Joseph Jordan, Sir John Harman, and Sir John Kempthorne.
[*Cf.* Bodl. Rawlinson MSS. A. 185, f. 453.]

P. 185.—The Parliament's order for Mr. Pepys' general report of the state of the navy, 22 April, 1675, with the papers presented by him in pursuance thereof:
[See *Catalogue of Pepysian MSS.* i. 46. *Cf.* Bodl. Rawlinson MSS. A. 175, ff. 291-8.]

    P. 185.—A particular of the papers and survey book presented to the House of Commons by Mr. Pepys, . . . April 24, 1675. . . .

    P. 188.—A list of all his Majesty's ships and vessels, expressing the respective rates and qualities, with their several ages, burdens, number of men, and guns.

    P. 191.—Ships repaired and workmen employed in the several yards, April, 1675.

    P. 192.—Provisions in the victualling stores, 1 April, 1675.

    P. 193.—A list of his Majesty's fleet as the same stands this 24 April, 1675, consisting of men-of-war (carrying from 20 guns upwards) and fire-ships. [Abstracted in Derrick, *Memoirs of the Royal Navy,* p. 86.]

P. 194.—A list of the French fleet as the same was taken in the year 1673, consisting of men-of-war (carrying from 20 guns upwards) and fire-ships.

P. 196.—A list of the fleet of the United Provinces as the same was taken in the year 1673, consisting of men-of-war (carrying from 20 guns upwards) and fire-ships.

P. 198.—An abstract of the distinct numbers and force of the present fleets of England, France, and Holland compared, consisting of 20 guns and upwards. [Printed in *Catalogue of Pepysian MSS.* i. 46. *Cf.* MS. Nos. 2265-6 *supra,* Nos. 13, 70, 162.]

P. 211.—Captain Jenifer's letter giving an account of the Spanish West India fleet, 29 May, 1675.

P. 219.—Articles of agreement between the Kings of England and France relating to the union of their fleets, anno 1672.

P. 231.—The French King's commission to the Duke of York to be commander-in-chief of his fleet united with that of England, anno 1672.

P. 233.—The French King's commission to any commander-in-chief of the fleet of England in the absence of the Duke of York, Lord High Admiral, to have the command of his fleet, anno 1672.

P. 235.—A paper relating to salutes between their Majesties' fleets, 1 Feb., 1669[-70]. [*French.*]

P. 239.—Notes from one Mr. Jasper Goodman, a shipwright by trade, who had been three years a slave at Algiers, concerning the present state of that place as to their skill in building of ships, 22 June 1680.
[Another copy is in Bodl. Rawlinson MSS. A. 175, f. 317.]

P. 243-4.—Sir Anthony Deane's son's letter [9 Feb., 1675-6] to M. Sausigny, ordinary commissary at Toulon, about the galley-frigates, and Sir Anthony's memorandum relating thereto, with M. Sausigny's answer [11 April, 1676].
[See *Catalogue of Pepysian MSS.* i. 228. Another copy is in Bodl. Rawlinson MSS. A. 175, ff. 322-5.]

P. 244-257.—Mr. Pepys' enquiries to Mr. Shere about ship-building, and his answer [May, 1680].
[See Bodl. Rawlinson MSS. A 175, ff. 326-30.]

P. 259.—Commissioner Deane's observations upon the improvement of our frigates in sailing. [March, 1675.]
[*Cf.* Bodl. Rawlinson MSS. A. 175, f. 332.]

P. 267.—The royal navy of England, anno 1633.
[Printed, with omissions, in Derrick, *Memoirs of the Royal Navy,* p. 59.]

P. 271.—A particular list of the seamen, bargemen, fishermen, and watermen in every province of France, anno 1677.
[Abstracted in *Catalogue of Pepysian MSS.* i. 55. *Cf.* Bodl. Rawlinson MSS. A. 175, f. 336; 176, ff. 11*b,* 120.]

P. 279.—The navy of France, anno 1677.
[*Cf.* Bodl. Rawlinson MSS. A. 175, f. 340.]

P. 281.—An account of the galleys of France, their number and charge, with the names of their commanders, anno 1677.

P. 283.—A list of the French fleet abroad, anno 1673.

P. 291.—Byam's narrative of the state of Guiana as it stood anno 1665 . . . .
[Another copy is in Bodl. Rawlinson MSS. A. 175, f. 342. Lieut.-General William Byam was Governor of Guiana.]

P. 351.—Colonel Scott's history and description of the river of the Amazones, found among his papers.
[On John Scott, the adventurer, Pepys's accuser, see *D.N.B.* li. 41.]

P. 415.—Colonel Scott's preface to an intended history of America, found among his papers.

P. 483.—A list of the yearly salaries of officers belonging to the admiralty and navy; taken out of the admiralty office about one month before his Majesty's happy restoration.

P. 487.—Considerations tendered to the King by Sir Richard White, February 1684-5, concerning Jamaica and all our foreign plantations in America.

P. 499.—The case cf Mr. Rider stated in arithmetic and depending upon fractions; being a trial of skill in that science.

P. 503.—A note of all the havens in Spain . . . . with the like of Portugal, and a perfect note of all their shipping . . . ['Ex chartophyl. Cæsariense'].
[B.M. Lansdowne MSS. clxxi. 138, f. 261.]

P. 513.—A note of the musters of persons of all qualities in Spain, anno 1588.

P. 523.—Several considerations relating to trade, offered to the subjects of Great Britain in the year 1684, with some further speculations thereon by George Carew, Esq.
[A copy addressed to Pepys, and dated $\frac{12}{22}$ Sept., 1684, is in Bodl. Rawlinson MSS. A. 193, f. 152. *Cf.* also *Several Considerations offered to the Parliament concerning the improvement of Trade, etc.* [by George Carew], London, 1675.]

P. 551.—A list of the King of France's ships in the port of Brest, September 1684.

P. 555.—An account of the proceedings of the French King's fleet before Algiers, 1683. [*French.*]

P. 559.—Sir William Petty's arithmetical observations relating to the wealth, taxes, and public charges of the State.

P. 579.—A catalogue of all the King's ships . . . . December 1607.
[Another copy is in MS. No. 2870 (*Miscellanies* ii. 131).]

P. 583.—A collection of several lists and establishments shewing the various numbers of men at several times allowed to his Majesty's ships now in being, namely from anno 1651 to this instant, 1675.

P. 595.—A list of all ships, frigates, and other vessels belonging to the State's navy, 1 March 1651[-2].
[Printed, but not very accurately, in Derrick, *Memoirs of the Royal Navy,* pp. 69-74.]

P. 599.—A list of the new frigates built by the Parliament from 1646 to 1653.
[Abstracted in Derrick, *Memoirs of the Royal Navy,* p. 237.]

P. 603.—Journal of the proceedings of the East India Company's ship Return upon the coast of Japan, 29 June to 28 August 1673 . . . .

P. 623.—A commission granted upon the death of the Duke of Buckingham to the Lord Weston and others to execute the office of Lord High Admiral of England, Ireland, Wales, etc., 20 September, 1628.

P. 631.—The King's commission to the Lord Weston and others to execute the office of Lord High Admiral of England, Wales, etc., 20 November 1632.

P. 639.—The King's commission to the Earl of Lindsey and others to execute the office of Lord High Admiral of England, Wales, etc., 10 April 1635.

[Another copy is in MS. 2874 (*Miscellanies* vi. 111).]

P. 645.—A memorandum relating to another commission to William, Lord Bishop of London, and others, 16 March 1635[-6].

P. 647.—A commission to the Earl of Lindsey to be admiral, custos maris, captain-general, and governor of a particular fleet then setting forth, 14 May, 1635.

P. 655.—A similar commission to Algernon, Earl of Northumberland, 23 March 1635[-6].

P. 662.—A memorandum relating to a like commission granted to the Earl of Northumberland, 30 March 1637.

Volume VI [2874]

[pp. 592, including table of contents.]

Copies of 65 miscellaneous documents, the greater part of which are *temp.* Car. II. These include :

P. 1–30.—Papers relating to Sir William Petty's "new-built sluice-bottomed vessel," 1684.

[*Cf.* MS. No. 2870 (*Miscellanies* ii. 489-503). A letter on the subject from Sir William Petty to Pepys, dated 3 July, 1683, is printed in *The Life, Journals, and Correspondence of Samuel Pepys* i. 322, London, 1841.]

P. 31.—Sir William Petty's Essay in Political Arithmetic concerning the multiplication of mankind.

P. 35.—Sir William Petty's letter to Sir John Werden touching a travelling chariot, 1 Jan., 1684-5.

P. 43–5.—The establishment touching the rights of the Lord High Admiral in time of hostility, 6 March 1665-6, with an explanation of 24 March 1667-8.

P. 47–74.—A collection of papers containing all the several establishments for relief of persons sick and wounded [1672], and the widows, orphans, etc., of them that were slain in the King's service at sea [1673]; rewards to sea-officers wounded in fight [1673-4]; and the standing rules of relief ordinarily allowed to mariners and soldiers maimed in his Majesty's service at sea out of their public chest at Chatham [24 July, 1685.]

[*Cf.* MS. No. 2266, *supra*, No. 136; MS. No. 2867 (*Naval Precedents*, pp. 335, 536 *et seqq.*); No. 2902 (*Day Collection*, p. 67); MS. No. 2879 (*Miscellanies* xi. 103-110); and see *Catalogue of Pepysian MSS.* i. 132. The 'rules of relief' are printed in *ib.* i. 139.]

P. 99.—Extract of the several contracts for victualling the navy from 1612 to 1660, together with an abstract of the victuallers' accounts between 1625 and 1642.

P. 107.—A commission granted by the admiral of Scotland for the arming out a privateer against the States of Holland [5 April] 1672.

P. 111.—A commission granted to Robert, Earl of Lindsey, and others to execute the office of Lord High Admiral of England [10 April], 11 Car. I. [Another copy is in MS. No. 2873 (*Miscellanies*, v. 639).]

P. 119.—The King's letters patents to the Earl of Northumberland for the office of Lord High Admiral of England, 13 April, 14 Car. I. [*Latin.*]

P. 135.—The King's letters patents to John Gill for the office of marshal in the southern parts of Cornwall, 10 February, 1682[-3]. [*Latin.*]

P. 137.—The King's commission under the great seal of England to Sir Leoline Jenkins for the office of judge of the high court of admiralty, 20 February, 1 Jac. II. [*Latin.*]
[*Cf.* p. 197 below.]

P. 147.—The King's letters patents to Henry Fauconberg, Doctor at Laws, for the office of judge of the vice-admiralty in the county of Norfolk, 28 September, 1681. [*Latin.*]

P. 153.—Statutes and ordinances for all vice-admirals and under-officers of the admiralty within the realm.

P. 159.—The King's letters patents to Sir Joseph Tredenham for the office of vice-admiral in the northern parts of Cornwall, etc., 24 November, 1679. [*Latin.*]

P. 171.—The King's letters patents to the Duke of Grafton to be vice-admiral and lieutenant-general of the admiralty of England, 30 January, 34 Car. II.
[*Cf.* a better copy, but dated 13 Jan., in MS. No. 2867 (*Naval Precedents,* p. 40).]

P. 175.—The commissioners of the admiralty's warrant to Sir Leoline Jenkins for a patent to Mr. Herbert to be rear-admiral of England, etc., 22 January 1683-4.

P. 177.—The King's letters patent to Mr. Herbert to be rear-admiral of England, etc., 22 January, 1683[-4].
[*Cf.* MS. No. 2867, (*Naval Precedents,* p. 42), in which this document is recited.]

P. 181.—The King's commission to Sir Richard Lloyd to be advocate-general, 12 February 1684-5.

P. 183.—The King's letters patents to William Joynes, gentleman, for the office of marshal of the admiralty, 5 March, 1684-5. [*Latin.*]
[*Cf.* MS. No. 2867 (*Naval Precedents,* p. 269).]

P. 185.—The King's letters patents to John Bowler for the office of register of the vice-admiralty in the county of Southampton and Isle of Wight, 27 March, 1685. [*Latin.*]

P. 187.—The King's letters patents to Mr. Thomas Bedford granting him the reversion of the office of register of the admiralty after the death of Sir Orlando Gee, etc., 15 April, 1685. [*Latin.*]
[*Cf.* MS. No. 2867 (*Naval Precedents*), p. 268.]

P. 191.—The King's letters patents to Henry Stiles, Doctor at Laws, for the office of judge of the admiralty of Ireland, 1 July, 1685. [*Latin.*]

P. 197-9.—The King's warrant for a commission under the great seal of England to Sir Leoline Jenkins to be judge of the high court of admiralty, 19 February 1684[-5], with a memorandum and docquet.
[*Cf.* p. 137 above.]

E

P. 203.—The institution of the hospital founded by Sir William Boreman at Greenwich for the maintenance and bringing up of twenty seamen's sons of that place in the art of navigation.
[Sir William Boreman was clerk of the Green Cloth to Charles II.]

P. 211–16.—The King's warrant and draft of the foundation of a marine hospital designed about Limehouse, Wapping, etc., 4 April 1684, with the 'paper of heads' there referred to.

P. 217.—A paper relating to the hospital propounded to be built for seamen and their male children to be bred to the sea, 1 January 1684[-5].

P. 221.—A list of the ships belonging to Sallee, 17 February 1684-5.

P. 233.—Extract of Consul Goodwin's letter from Tunis relating to the present naval force, with the names of ships, commanders, etc., belonging to that Government, 1 August 1685.

P. 235.—A copy of instructions to Mr. Carver, going in the ship Francis, an interloper, to the East Indies, 20 Sept., 1684.

P. 243–57.—Papers relating to the Shipwrights' Company [1684-5].

P. 259.—Establishment and regulation of rewards for his Majesty's land-forces, 1685.

P. 263.—The general list of the French fleet, anno 1685.

P. 267.—Mr. Erlisman, consul for the King of Great Britain at Algiers, his list of all men-of-war belonging to that Government, 1 June 1685.
[*Cf.* MS. No. 2875 (*Miscellanies* vii. 497) and MS. No. 2879 (*Miscellanies* xi. 97).]

P. 271.—Captain Bartholomew Sharpe's journal during his being in the South Seas, etc., anno 1680.
[See MS. No. 2610 *supra*, p. 1.]

P. 333.—Ditto, from the Gulf of Adulce on the coast of Rico to the south, 1681.
[See MS. No. 2610 *supra*, p. 62.]

P. 361.—Notes preparative to the navy officers' following defence upon the several observations and exceptions of the commissioners for accounts sitting at Brook House.

P. 385.—The navy officers' defence, being a journal of what passed between the commissioners of accounts and myself before his Majesty in council touching their reports and observations upon Sir George Carteret and the navy office; as also the pretended diversion of moneys to other uses than the wars.
[See *Catalogue of Pepysian MSS.* i. 32-6, 142-3.]

P. 509.—Mr. Pepys' defence of the proceedings of the officers of the navy and himself in reference to the late war, with his several letters accompanying copies thereof to the King and Duke, anno 1669.
[This is another copy of MS. No. 2554.]

P. 591.—An establishment of the certain measure for beating the English march in all services, domestic and foreign, by the drummers of this nation, by King Charles I, 1631 . . . .

Volume VII [2875]

[pp. 509 + pp. 16 table of contents.]

Copies of 168 miscellaneous documents, mainly *temp.* P. and M., Eliz., and Jac. I, and all transcribed 'ex chartophylacio Regio.' These include the following :

P. 1.—A collection of payments made to the navy between February 1537[-8] and June, 1541, taken out of the original book of accounts (for that time) of Sir Brian Tuke, treasurer of the King's chamber, remaining in the Library of the Royal Society, London.

P. 10-50.—Papers of 1557-8 relating mainly to naval preparations.
[A list of ships of 29 May, 1557, given on p. 13, is printed, with certain omissions, in Derrick, *Memoirs of the Royal Navy,* p. 19.]

P. 60.—A parallel of the charge, ordinary and extraordinary, before the year 1679 and that of the five years following in relation to the navy.

P. 61.—A copy of a letter to the four principal officers of the navy requiring them to lie alternatively on board of her Majesty's ships to see the same well guarded, 22 March 1584[-5].

P. 62.—A note shewing the advantage that might accrue to her Majesty and country from the increase of seamen's wages, etc. Dec., 1585.

P. 63.—A list of the Low Country ships, with their men and tonnage, 24 June, 1588.

P. 110.—A certificate of all manner of shipping in the Cinque Ports, as it was 8 March 1562[-3] and 30 years before.

P. 115.—A list of ships built since the beginning of the year 1571 to 10 March 1575[-6].

P. 117.—A note of the services done for the advancement of the navy since Michaelmas, 1579.

P. 126.—A view taken by the officers and master-shipwrights of the navy of such timber-trees as are growing in the Queen's forests therein-mentioned fit for the repair of her Majesty's ships, 14 Aug., 1593.

P. 127.—Her Majesty's commission to Sir Francis Drake, Sir John Hawkyns, Sir Thomas Gorge, and Sir Thomas Barkewith to provide against an invasion from Spain, 11 August 1595.
[See *Sir Francis Drake, his Voyage,* 1595, by Thomas Maynarde (Hakluyt Society, 1849).]

P. 140.—A proposition shewing how England might be the staple for cordage to be sent therefrom into all parts of Europe.

P. 145.—Articles touching the survey of her Majesty's ships, as also for the enquiry of abuses heretofore committed, and to set down remedies for preventing of the same.
[A brief form of commission authorising an enquiry since the year 1579.]

P. 158.—Certain articles delivered to her Majesty against John Hawkyns about matters relating to the navy, 10 October 1587.
[*Cf.* S.P. Domestic Eliz. cciv. 16-18 and B.M. Lansdowne MSS. lii. 43.]

P. 183.—The commissioners of the navy's report concerning Sir Robert Mansell's accounts, 25 February 1619[-20].
[This is in S.P. Dom. Jac. I. cxii. 101.]

P. 203.—A survey of the state of his Majesty's ships at Chatham taken 31 August, 1624.

    [Noted in Derrick, *Memoirs of the Royal Navy*, p. 53.]

P. 220.—The opinion of several able sea-captains whether it be best for the fleet (consisting of 30 English ships and 20 Dutch) to lie on our coast to guard it, or to go to the coast of Spain to hinder their preparations and joining, 10 June, 1626.

P. 223.—Reasons why the King's ships should be graved when they go to sea, Sept. 1627.

P. 226-35.—Certificates of the commissioners, etc., concerning the worm at Portsmouth, 1630.

P. 252.—Copy of Mr. Manwell's petition and project to keep a registry of seamen, ships, ordnance, etc., 29 Oct., 1634.

P. 270-6.—Eight questions presented to the lords of the admiralty by John Hollond, paymaster of the navy, 29 Nov., 1636.

P. 273.—Inconveniencies attending payments to wrong parties in the navy office, though upon tickets fully signed and warranted, [by John Hollond], 1636.

P. 303.—Copy of his Majesty's contract with Sir Allen Apsley and Sir Sampson Darell, surveyors of his Majesty's marine victuals, anno 1622[-3]. [9 Jan.]

    [*Cf.* also pp. 380, 381.]

P. 317.—Order bearing date 22 Dec., 1626, for the former commissioners of the navy to survey the same, etc.

P. 354-60.—A note of the ancient salary of the principal and subordinate officers of the navy, with the increase made to divers of them since their first institution, etc., anno 1634 [with a petition for increase, 8 Dec., 1635].

P. 361.—Sir William Monson's paper of propositions for the regulating divers evils in the navy, 12 Jan., 1635[-6].

P. 368-79.—Papers relating to the making of a haven at Hastings [1636].

P. 382.—Reasons given by Mr. Hollond why the master shipwright should not keep a private yard, 9 Aug., 1652.

    [Discussed in Hollond's *Discourses of the Navy*, p. xxiii. Another copy is in State Papers Domestic, Interr. xxiv. 97.]

P. 388.—Articles to be enquired into by the commissioners for the survey of the state of the navy [1626?].

P. 390.—A paper presented to the lords of the council concerning navigation, building of ships, etc.

P. 401.—A project for the sea in opposition to Spain [Eliz.].

P. 415.—An abstract of the account of the Chest at Chatham for 20 years [1617-37].

    [*Cf.* also pp. 398, 399.]

P. 421-63.—An account of all the proceedings had in the years 1683 and 1684 between the Brotherhood of Free Shipwrights of London and the new Corporation of Shipwrights of Redrith.

    [*Cf.* Bodl. Rawlinson MSS. A. 177, ff. 166-220, ' Papers relating to the new Company of Shipwrights of Redrith or Rotherhithe and their charters. . . *c.* 1605-1688.']

P. 465.—The journal of the Green Ribband Club at the King's Head Tavern over against the Temple in Fleet Street from 1678 to 1681.

    [' Copied from the original lent me by the King.']

P. 493-5.—A proposition of one Anthony De Gerente, alias Clerant, to his Majesty, about a composition of tar for preserving wood and cordage. [*French.*]

P. 497.—An account of the number, force, and figures in the sterns of all the present corsairs of Algiers, 7 September 1685.
[*Cf.* MS. No. 2874 (*Miscellanies* vi. 267) and MS. No. 2879 (*ib.* xi. 97).]

P. 499.—Captain Nevill's letter giving an account by way of journal of the proceedings of the French fleet against Algiers, annis 1682 and 1683.

Volume VIII [2876]

[pp. 720 + pp. 16 table of contents.]

Copies of 274 documents, being "an entire transcript of Sir Robert Cotton's volume of sea affairs and expeditions from King Henry VIII to King James I, under the title of Otho E. 9 . . ." The volume is used by Derrick (*Memoirs of the Royal Navy*, pp. 6, 14-16, 20, 23, 29, 34). Many of the papers relate to the Spanish Armada and a few to Admiralty affairs. They include :

P. 1.—A list of the Admirals from 48 Henry III to 27 Elizabeth. [*Latin.*]
[B.M. Cott. MSS. Otho E ix, 1.]

P. 135.—A note of all the ports, and creeks to them belonging, within the realm of England and Wales, *temp.* Hen. VIII.
[*Cf.* B.M. Cott. MSS. Otho E ix, f. 76.]

P. 161.—An indenture between her Majesty and Edward Baeshe, surveyor-general of the victuals, relating to the victualling of her navy, 13 April, 1564.
[*Cf.* B.M. Cott. MSS. Otho E ix, ff. 58, 90, 106. See also pp. 171-2.]

P. 207.—The rates of wages of all officers in every her Majesty's ship, December 1587.

P. 235.—An abstract of a certificate made to the council of all ships and other vessels belonging to the Five Ports and members thereof, together with the number of able masters and mariners appertaining thereto, 1587.
[B.M. Cott. MSS. Otho E ix, f. 142; printed in Charnock, *Marine Architecture,* ii. 129.]

P. 237.—The number of ships throughout the realm collected out of the certificate thereof returned in the year 1588.
[B.M. Cott. MSS. Otho E ix, f. 144; printed in Charnock, *Marine Architecture*, ii. 131. Mr. Oppenheim thinks that it is wrongly dated (*The Administration of the Royal Navy,* pp. 175-6.]

P. 269.—A device how to secure the river of Thames against the attempts of foreign galleys, to be executed by Sir Henry Palmer, April, 1600.
[B.M. Cott. MSS. Otho E ix, 162 *b.*; printed in Charnock, *Marine Architecture,* ii. 133. In 1600 Sir Henry Palmer, then comptroller of the navy, was in command of the defences of the Thames (*D.N.B.* xliii. 128).]

P. 297-307.—An abstract of the whole fleet set forth anno 1588 against the Spanish Armada [and various lists of ships].
[*Cf.* B.M. Cott. MSS. Otho E ix, f. 175, and Laughton, *Defeat of the Spanish Armada,* ii. 323 (*N.R.S.* Publications, vol. ii).]

P. 325.—An estimate of the charge of her Majesty's army prepared against the Spaniards, from the beginning of November, 1587, to the last of September, 1588; together with that of the coasters and voluntary ships paid by her Majesty, over and above the charge borne by London and the port towns throughout the realm, Oct., 1588.
[B.M. Cott. MSS. Otho E ix, f. 191.]

P. 344.—A proposal (made in the time of Queen Elizabeth) of a method to be established for the examining and admitting of mariners and pilots.

P. 351.—An account of mariners prested and resting unprested in the several counties of England, 23 April 1590.

P. 354.—The number of masters, mariners, and fishermen belonging to every shire throughout the realm, and wherrymen on the Thames, 1583.
[B.M. Cott. MSS. Otho E ix, f. 221; printed in Charnock, *Marine Architecture,* ii. 128.]

P. 368.—Several memorandums, directions, etc., relating to public matters, and chiefly Spain, all writ in my Lord Burghley's own hand, 1590.

P. 388–93, 397, 401–8.—Papers relating to the victualling of the navy, 1590.

P. 394.—A list of all the ships and other vessels of her Majesty's fleet, with their number of men, mariners, gunners, and soldiers, 26 Feb., 1589[-90].

P. 415.—A certificate of ships and vessels in the ports and towns of Essex, Suffolk, Norfolk, Kent, and Sussex, anno 1591.
[B.M. Cott. MSS. Otho E ix, f. 262; printed in Charnock, *Marine Architecture,* ii. 148.]

P. 551.—A list of ships built in the several ports of England since 33 Elizabeth, with their burden and allowance from her Majesty towards the same, 1597.

P. 612.—Articles towards the amendment of the victualler's contract, dated Feb. 1611[-12].

P. 632.—A memorial for preventing undue proceedings in the making of contracts for provisions for the navy, and other abuses, all written in the Lord Burghley's own hand.

P. 644.—The true discipline of the navy and duty of the officers thereof, set down by Sir Robert Cotton.

P. 669.—The names and duties of every of the then officers of his Majesty's navy, Sir Robert Mansell being treasurer, Sir Henry Palmer comptroller, Sir John Trevor surveyor, and P. Buck clerk thereof.

Volume IX [2877]

[pp. 473, including pp. 10 tables of contents.]

Copies of 100 documents being 'A Collection of Papers and Notes upon the subject of the Dominion and Sovereignty of the British Seas, the right of the flag, and matters relating to salutes and colours." A note at the end of the volume refers to *Miscellanies* iv. 237 for 'much more matter upon the same subject with this volume, viz. : sea-dominion, right of the flag, salutes, and colours.' The papers bearing on Sea Dominion include :

P. 2–115.—Sir Philip Meadows's observations touching the dominion and sovereignty of the seas, with his original letter to Mr. Secretary Pepys accompanying the same.

[See also pp. 465-70. The 'original letter,' dated 2 Jan., 1686[-7], is inserted opposite p. 115. On this important work, published in 1689, see Fulton, *The Sovereignty of the Sea*, pp. 524-7. A transcript of the Pepysian MS. is in B.M. Add. MSS. 30221.]

and a number of documents [pp. 137, 187, 197, 227, 235-40, 259-60, 275, 285, 295, 319-22, 369, 447-54] relating to the practice of striking to the King's flag.

The papers relating to salutes and to the history of the flag are catalogued in full as follows:

SALUTES

P. 189.—Copies of the 32nd and 38th articles of the general printed instructions annexed to the commanders of his Majesty's ships' commissions touching salutes.

P. 195.—Second instructions to his Majesty's officers at sea touching salutes. ['Received from Mr. Brisbane, 22 May, 1681.']

P. 199-226, 231-234.—Papers relating to 'salutes between us and Spain, both at sea and in ports' [p. 231], 1683.

P. 229-30.—Papers relating to salutes at Genoa, 1681 and 1683.

P. 241.—'Loose notes about salutes at Livorne, under Secretary Jenkins's own hand,' 2 March 1680-1.

P. 267.—Notes upon the business of salutes, as they stand in the present practice of the navy, 1684.

P. 303.—To the Governor of Portsmouth about salutes to ships, 20 May, 1674.

P. 305.—An abstract of the rules about the flag and topsail and salutes by guns at this day established and observed by the King's ships at home and abroad with respect to those of foreign princes, 25 Jan. 1684-5.

P. 307.—Materials towards a settlement of the business of salutes between us and Spain, 1684.

P. 309.—A paper concerning salutes offered by somebody to his Royal Highness, and by him put into the hands of Mr. Pepys, Jan., 1684-5.

THE HISTORY OF THE FLAG

P. 261.—The King's proclamation declaring what flags South and North Britain shall bear at sea [12 April, 1606].

[This proclamation is summarised in *Bibliography of Tudor and Stuart Proclamations* (Bibliotheca Lindesiana), Oxford, 1910, i. p. 120, No. 1032. Opposite p. 262 are inserted a pen-and-ink drawing on paper of the standard used at the funeral of the Lord Kinloss, Master of the Rolls, 17 Feb., 1611[-12], and an illumination on vellum of a standard of a similar type.]

P. 263.—Mr. Bedford's references to authors upon the flag, 11 April 1685.

[Mr. Bedford was register of the admiralty.]

P. 265.—Mr. Joynes, marshal of the admiralty, his account of the time when the custom-house wherries first were permitted to carry the jack in their sterns, it being in the King's first Dutch war to exempt them from pressing, 22 September 1686.

P. 270.—The form of the flags provided by Sir William Dugdale for the yachts that transported the Prince and Princess to Holland presently after their marriage, November 1677.

[These are coloured drawings on paper of the flag borne on the Charlotte with the Prince, and that borne on the Mary with the Princess.]

P. 271.—The King's proclamation for regulating the colours to be worn on merchant-ships, 18 September 1674.

[See p. 437 below. The proclamation is summarised in *Bibliography of Tudor and Stuart Proclamations* (Bibliotheca Lindesiana), i. p. 435, No. 3599.]

P. 277.—Captain Akerman to Mr. Pepys touching the unadvisableness of the custom-house boats wearing the King's jack, 23 October, 1685.

P. 279.—Notes taken from Captain Locke touching custom-house jacks, November 1685.

P. 281.—Copy of Mr. Brisbane's letter to Colonel Wyndham touching his carrying the jack in his yacht [5 June, 1685].

[Mr. Brisbane was judge-advocate of the fleet.]

P. 313.—Ordonnance pour le port des pavillons d'amiral, vice-amiral, et contr'amiral, 24 Aout, 1665 [with a translation].

P. 315.—Notes about the jack taken by S.P. at the navy board, 20 September, 1686, upon occasion of the liberty taken by private yachts to wear the King's jack without licence.

P. 329.—A note touching a jack worn by a private yacht, and the dishonour done thereto on board the said yacht, 1686.

P. 331.—Sir Roger Strickland's letter from the Bay of Bulls, dated 22 September, 1686, to Mr. Pepys giving an account of his proceeding thither in 16 days from England, and complaining of Captain Preistman's wearing an extraordinary swallow-tailed pendant or flag, and lying there with the galley to take in money.

[See *Catalogue of Pepysian MSS.* i. 211.]

P. 333.—A comparison of the flags and pendants (number 1, 2, 3) ordinarily borne by his Majesty's ships, with that extraordinary one of Captain Preistman's (number 4) complained of in Sir Roger Strickland's foregoing letter [with a memorandum of 1 April, 1687].

[Four coloured drawings of the flags are given.]

P. 336-54.—A collection of papers passing between Sir Roger Strickland and Mr. Pepys relating to his claim to wear the union flag at the fore-topmast head [May-July, 1687].

P. 365.—What Captain Young and others remember concerning the colours worn by the flag-ships and merchantmen in the reign of King Charles I. Collected by Mr. Hunter at my desire and owned by Captain Young upon reading the same, 27 April 1687.

P. 367.—The dimensions of the ordinary ensigns, flags, jacks, and pendants of his Majesty's ships of each rate; with the like of the distinction pendant used in the Downs [1676].

[On the 'distinction pendant' see *Catalogue of Pepysian MSS.* iii. 209 (*N.R.S.* Publications, vol. xxxvi).]

P. 368.—Memorandums for enquiry and entry about flags, September 1687.

P. 370.—Instances [*temp*. Henr. VIII] of the sea-whistle or call worn by the Lord High Admirals of England as the ensign of their office.

P. 371.—King James I his proclamation declaring what flags South and North Britains shall bear at sea, 12 April 1606.

P. 371.—An abstract of the intended establishment about flags, as it was first designed and resolved on by the King, though not yet put into execution by any solemn formal act, with a memorandum of 4 April, 1687.

P. 372.—The signals appointed by the instructions for fighting and sailing, with the placings thereof.

[The purpose of the various signals is set out in tabular form. *Cf.* Corbett, *Fighting Instructions*, p. 152 (*N.R.S.* Publications, vol. xxix).]

P. 375–401.—Notes upon the doctrine of flags and colours of distinction at sea in the royal navy of England, apart both from that of the merchants' service and the King's own not relating to his navy.

P. 376.—Sub-notes about flags and colours.

P. 380.—Notes towards the finishing the establishment about flags.

P. 381.—Notes about colours used in the royal navy, as to sorts and dimensions.

P. 385.—A distribution of every sort of ship and vessel employed in the King's service according to their several distinct circumstances, leading to a determination which shall and which shall not carry the King's jack.

P. 386.—An application of the several flags used in the royal navy of England on occasions purely honorary.

P. 388.—Designs of distinction for the vice- and rear-admirals of England, by Sir Roger Strickland.

[Coloured drawings of flags on thin pasteboard inserted.]

P. 391.—A designation of the several flags and colours used in the royal navy of England for distinguishing degrees of command therein.

[A table on thin pasteboard inserted. This is followed by four blank pages, and a memorandum on p. 399, ' That the foregoing collection of notes and papers (from page 371) relating to flags and colours, had by the beginning of the year 1688 been so far advanced and considered by the King as to have wanted very little of being brought under a formal establishment . . . . when by the interruption arising to that and many other matters of general reglement then on foot, upon intelligence of the extraordinary sea-preparations making in Holland, the same was wholly, and by the general issue thereof at the end of the year finally, prevented : saving only in the two particulars' of minor importance set out in the memorandum itself.]

P. 402.—A discourse written by Mr. Serjeant Knight, serjeant-chirurgeon to King Charles II, at the desire of Mr. Pepys . . . containing the history of the cross of St. George, and its becoming the sole distinction-flag, badge, or cognizance of England by sea and land.

[Mr. Knight's original letter, dated 12 Jan., 1677-8, is inserted. There are coloured drawings of flags in the margins of pp. 412, 417, 418, 419, 420, and 435; and a coloured genealogy of the Kings of England on p. 425.]

P. 427.—Mr. Serjeant Knight's prospect of a fleet in three squadrons distinguished by the colours of St. George.

[An ink and coloured drawing of a fleet on two thicknesses of paper, quarto, inserted to illustrate a reference on p. 422.]

P. 430.—Mr. Serjeant Knight's proposal of diverse methods of disposing of St. George's cross under the colours of distinction proper to the several squadrons, together with his device for the Standard of England made up with the cross of Ulster in lieu of the harp for Ireland, and his conception touching a method for the bearing of the cross of St. George by merchants' ships.

[Coloured drawings of flags on four pages thin paper, quarto, inserted to illustrate a reference on p. 422.]

P. 437.—King Charles II's proclamation for regulating the colours to be worn by merchants' ships, 18 September, 1674 [*printed*].

[See p. 271 above.]

P. 439.—Mr. Sandford, late Lancaster herald, his letter to the Bishop of Ely containing his exception to Signor Vario's painting St. George in the great hall at Windsor without his shield and cross.

[There are coloured drawings of flags and coats of arms on pp. 440, 441, 442, 443, 445. Sandford resigned his office in 1689 and died in 1694. Signor Verrio, the King's painter, was associated with Pepys in connexion with Christ's Hospital, where he painted the large picture in the Hall representing Charles II delivering the charter to the Royal Mathematical School (Pearce, *Annals of Christ's Hospital,* pp. 56, 103, 133, 134*n.*]

P. 471.—A proclamation, 12 July 1694, concerning colours to be worn on board ships [*printed*].

[This proclamation is summarised in *Bibliography of Tudor and Stuart Proclamations* (Bibliotheca Lindesiana) i. p. 495, No. 4138.]

P. 472B.—My observation upon the lowness of the place assigned by the Earl Marshal to the banner of union among the nine banners borne in the funeral-proceeding for the Queen by them made 5 March, 1694-5 [with a printed copy of the form of proceeding at Queen Mary's funeral inserted.]

Volume X [2878]

[pp. 733 + pp. 12 table of contents.]

Copies of 185 documents. Of these, pp. 1–204, and 367, 407, 524, relate almost entirely to the affairs of the ordnance, *temp.*, Edw. VI., Eliz. and Jac. I.; pp. 360, 364, 369, 393, 399, 405, 411, 415, 421, 424, 521, 525, 528, 529, 530, 531, 533, 539, 545, 547, 549, 551, 559, 565, 568, 591, and 596, relate to cordage, hemp, and masts.

Another group of papers relate to shipbuilding, including "A paper arguing for building ships for the King by contract as anno 1589" [p. 505]; see also pp. 685–704, 'A Discourse concerning Sea Dominion':

Begins: 'That free and absolute princes may have propriety in the dominion of the seas coasting upon their territories . . . '

and pp. 705–24, 'Arguments proving the King's exclusive propriety of dominion in the seas coasting on his kingdoms, both as to passage and fishing therein,'

> *Begins* : 'Concerning the peculiar interest and propriety of his Majesty in his sovereignty over the seas of his several kingdoms. . . . '

with various papers relating to fishery rights, pp. 627–84.

The following documents relate to abuses in the navy. Some of them are described and discussed in the introduction to Hollond's *Discourses*, pp. xxxiii-liii (*N.R.S.* Publications, vol. vii).]

P. 226–56.—A large and severe discourse concerning several abuses in the navy, Chatham, 1597.

> [Chiefly complaints against minor officials. *Begins* : 'If ever any wrong or cruel and most vile dealing were offered to any prince in the world. . .']

P. 257–262.—A large and particular complaint against Phineas Pett, relating to abuses in the navy about the end of the Queen's and beginning of King James's reign.

> [The complainant, who writes in the first person, has a personal grudge against Pett. The paper begins, 'In the last year of the Queen's reign, I, seeing some abuses by Phineas Pett, I told him he had not done his duty. He stroke me with his cudgel. I told him he had been better he had held his hand, for he should pay for it. . . .']

P. 263–273.—Particular abuses to be proved against the officers of the navy about the same time [Jac. I].

> [Abuses in connexion with timber, masts, oil, tar, canvas, sea-pay, etc.]

P. 273–290.—A declaration of the omissions and abuses committed in the office of the navy about the same time [end of Eliz.].

> [Abuses in connexion with false entries and surcharges; urges an enquiry.]

P. 291–5.—Observations concerning some late abuses committed both by the principal and inferior officers of the navy, 6 July, 1611.

P. 296–8.—A letter relating to some other abuses in the victualling of ships and otherwise at Chatham, wages of workmen, etc., about the same time.

P. 299–302.—Notes of the same time to be remembered in the reformation of abuses in the offices of his Majesty's navy.

> [*Begins:* 'The better that the subject is paid, the better pennyworth shall his Majesty have, which may in part be reformed as follows. . . .']

P. 303–327.—More notes about the same time of the chief disorders to be reformed in the navy.

> [Abuses relating to the four principal officers in general, the victuallers, clerks of the check, storekeepers, captains at sea, pursers, boatswains, and gunners.]

P. 328–37.—Particular abuses complained of against Christopher Baker about timber and plank. *Temp*. R. Eliz.

P. 338–41.—Memorandum for reformation of the foregoing abuses.

P. 342–3.—More informations of abuses in the navy, anno 1589.

> [Abuses by one Thomas Massingham, a ropemaker.]

P. 349–52.—Discoveries offered to the Queen by Thomas Wiggs concerning abuses in the admiralty, 1599.

[Charges of false entries and fraud; urges further enquiry.]

P. 371–2.—Thomas Norreys's letter to Sir Robert Cotton concerning examination of witnesses about irregularities in the navy, 21 Feb., 1607[-8].

[On the enquiry of 1608 see Oppenheim, *The Administration of the Royal Navy,* p. 193.]

P. 373–4.—Sir Robert Cotton's letter in behalf of Sir John Trevor, who owns and begs pardon for his unjust dealings, 12 May 1608.

P. 375–7.—P. Buck's letter to the Earl of Northampton mentioning some cheats used by boatswains and others in the King's service, 2 June 1608.

P. 378–9.—Thomas Buck's letter about plank bought of the Lord Worcester, anchors, and other matters, 2 Oct. 1608, with particular reflections on Sir Richard Hawkyns.

P. 380–3.—Thomas Buck's letter to Sir Robert Cotton complaining of several abuses in the King's navy, etc., 1 Feb. 1608[-9].

[The abuses referred to are in connexion with stores, victualling, and under-manning.]

P. 384–5.—P. Buck's letter to the Earl of Northampton showing the unreasonableness of giving the charge and keeping of the remains of nails to Samuel Maplesden, and entering him into wages on that account, etc., 15 Feb., 1608[-9].

P. 386–90.—P. Buck's letter to the Earl of Northampton complaining of Sir Robert Mansell's abusing him for excepting against his accounts, etc., 1 Aug., 1609.

P. 391–2.—Bills excepted against by Peter Buck that were passed at London by Sir Henry Palmer and Sir John Trevor, 26 Dec., 1609.

P. 400–4.—Advices given towards the regulating of his Majesty's navy, May, 1605.

P. 427–42.—Abuses and ill-husbandries exercised upon the bringing-in ships to be repaired in dry dock; with a large particular of other great abuses in the navy [Jac. I].

[Abuses connected with ships in harbour; with notes about complements, sea-stores, and pay in ships at sea.]

P. 443–5.—Reasons why the officers of the navy cannot with safety to themselves take an oath for true vouchers, if the allowances be passed, as they now are and of long time have been; with a hint of many considerable abuses relating thereto [Jac. I].

P. 455–8.—A very particular note of charges which may yearly be saved in the navy, without any impediment to the service [Jac. I].

P. 459–61.—Abuses in the business of measuring of the merchant ships by the King's officer, in order to their demand of tonnage from the King [Jac. I].

P. 462.—A letter showing the necessity of reforming abuses in the navy, and the inconveniences of giving liberty to the principal officers thereof to sell their places [Jac. I].

P. 471–2.—Christopher Baker's proposals for reformation of the navy.

[*Cf.* S.P. Dom. Eliz. ccxxii. 48.]

P. 494–8.—Thomas Wiggs's letter to the Earl of Leicester . . . complaining of cheats of Sir John Hawkyns's, 6 Feb., 1587[-8].

P. 501-4.—Thomas Wiggs's letter to the Earl of Leicester about his suit against Sir John Hawkyns, and other matters wherein he desires his lordship's assistance, 4 Feb. 1587[-8].

P. 733.—Wages paid by Sir Robert Mansell's clerk unto Sir William St. John's, and allowed upon the ship the Advantage for men supposed to have served; and done at the direction of the same clerk, without other testimony than the captain's and purser's vouchers, viz. from 16 June 1608 to 24 July 1609; with an estimate of the abuse suffered by the King therein.

Volume XI [2879]

[pp. 958 + pp. 12 table of contents, but pp. 285-393 have been taken out.]

Copies of 192 miscellaneous documents of various dates, the greater number being *temp*. Car. II and Jac. II. These include the following:

P. 1.—Resolutions taken at a conference held 17 April, 1686, between the commissioners of the navy and divers master-shipwrights touching the present condition of England in reference to plank for shipbuilding; with an order in council of 8 Oct., 1686, in approval of the same.
[The signatures of the master-shipwrights and the commissioners are carefully imitated. See also MS. No. 2867 (*Naval Precedents*, p. 215).]

P. 9.—An account of the fees or wages belonging to the Lord High Admiral and officers of the navy and ordnance in the time of Queen Elizabeth.
['From a MS. of Mr. Blathwait's of the Queen's time.']

P. 11.—The names of the forts and castles along the sea-coasts of England, and of the captains having the charge of them in the time of Queen Elizabeth.
['From a MS. of Mr. Blathwait's of the Queen's time.']

P. 13.—The naval force of the Crown of Sweden, October, 1688.

P. 18.—A state of the debt of the navy contracted between 1 January, 1671[-2] and 25 March, 1686.
[Printed in *Catalogue of Pepysian MSS*. i. 110.]

P. 27.—Extract out of the council-books containing the King's declaration about the future management of the three great offices of the Lord Treasurer, Lord Admiral, and Lord General. 7 January 1686-7.

P. 33-72.—Papers relating to the past and present practice of the ships of war of England in searching for and taking the subjects thereof out of any foreign ships [mainly 1688].

P. 73.—An entire copy of the instructions given by Edward Popham, Robert Blake, and Richard Deane, admiral and general of the fleet appointed by Parliament, to sea-commanders, April, 1650.

P. 97.—An account of the sea force of Algiers, August, 1687.
[Cf. MS. No. 2874 (*Miscellanies* vi. 267), and MS. No. 2875 (*ib*. vii, 497).]

P. 99.—Sir Joseph Williamson's note to Mr. Pepys out of the paper office touching the antiquity of the office of clerk of the navy, now clerk of the acts, 18 January, 1686-7.

P. 100.—The dimensions of the Margaret galley, built by Beneditto Carlini at Pisa, and presented to the King of England by the Great Duke, 1671.
[Noted in *Catalogue of Pepysian MSS*. i. 228n.]

P. 103–110.—The provision at this day made for relief of sick and wounded seamen under the management of James Pearse, Esq., chyrurgeon-general of the navy, and reported to me by him for the King's information in the following papers, Sept., 1687.

> [Discussed in *Catalogue of Pepysian MSS.* i. 137-8. *Cf.* MS. No. 2874 (*Miscellanies* vi. 47-74).]

P. 111.—A list of his Majesty's ships, with the number of guns proposed for each in time of war, 1 January, 1684-5.

> [Discussed in *Catalogue of Pepysian MSS.* i. 241-2.]

P. 122.—Abstract of the aforesaid state of ordnance, with an account how far the guns in store and on ship-board will comply with the same.

> [Part of this is printed in Derrick, *Memoirs of the Royal Navy*, p. 272.]

P. 123–132.—Order of the office of the ordnance for the march of the train of artillery, and instructions connected with the same.

P. 133–159.—Catalogus librorum MSS. Musaeo Ashmoleano legatorum a consultissimo antiquario domino Guilemo Dugdale, milite, Garterio Rege Armorum Anglicorum, A.D. 1685-6. . . . [*Latin.*]

P. 161.—A copy of the index to a volume of original letters and other papers (upon occasion of the Reformation) remaining in the library of the Dutch Church, London, and procured for my perusal by Mr. James Houblon, 1687. [*Latin.*]

P. 211.—The succession of the Lords High Admirals and general state of the office of the Lord High Admiral of England, from the murder of the Duke of Buckingham, 23 August 1628 (with whom Sir H. Spelman closes his list of admirals) to 18 December 1688, the day of King James's withdrawing and the Prince of Orange's entering upon the regency.

P. 227–9.—The present state of the shipping of Amsterdam, anno 1686. . . . .

P. 249.—The indictment, proceedings, and judgment in the case of Sir Edward Hales. . . . . [168 . .].

> [The proceedings in the collusive action of Godden *v.* Hales, which gave legal sanction to James II's claim that the dispensing power was part of the royal prerogative, lasted from 28 March until 21 June, 1686.]

P. 269.—The King's letters patents to Edward Seymour, Esq., to be treasurer of the navy, with £2,000 per annum salary, 5 July, 1673; with a privy seal for an additional £1,000 per annum, 17 July, 1674; and a grant of the said office to the Lord Falkland at £3,000 per annum, June, 1681. [*Latin.*]

P. 281.—Copies of three addresses to the King from the Trinity House upon the three great emergencies of state happening in the years 1681, 1682, and 1683, the first drawn by the Earl of Berkeley then master, and the two last by Mr. Pepys.

P. 394–561.—Papers relating to the conservancy of the Thames, and encroachments thereon [mainly 1684-5].

> [*Cf.* B.M. Cott. MSS. Otho. E. ix. f. 413, and Bodl. Rawlinson MSS. A. 171, f. 98.]

P. 562–912.—A collection of papers relating to the affairs of the Trinity House [1513-1687].

P. 913.—Sir Anthony Deane and Mr. Hewer their minutes of the proceedings at Chatham at his Majesty's visiting his yard and ships there, May, 1688, in order to the consulting for the safety of both, upon intelligence received of sea preparations extraordinary reported to be then making in Holland, with the different advices offered to the King thereupon, and issue of the whole.

P. 926–946.—A collection of papers containing the number, names, rates, built, age, dimensions, tonnage, complements of men and guns, and state of repair, of every ship and vessel of the royal navy of England, 18 December, 1688, being the day of King James II his withdrawing, and the determination of Mr. Pepys's relation thereto as secretary of the admiralty of England.

[Somewhat similar tables are printed in *Catalogue of Pepysian MSS.* i. 296-306, from a different source (MS. No. 2940).]

P. 947.—Table of rates of sea-wages per mensem . . . .

P. 951.—A particular of the public papers resting in the office of the secretary of the admiralty, 9 March, 1688-9, and since by him delivered over to the present commissioners for executing the office of the Lord High Admiral. [*Cf.* Bodl. Rawlinson MSS. A. 170, ff. 71-77.]

P. 954.—The receipt of Mr. Phineas Bowles (secretary to the commissioners of the admiralty) for the foregoing papers.

P. 955.—A particular of the public books resting in the office of the secretary of the admiralty of England 9 March, 1688-9, and since by him delivered over to the present commissioners for executing the office of the Lord High Admiral.

P. 958.—The receipt of Mr. Phineas Bowles for the foregoing books.

[P. 959.—The naval forces of the Czar of Muscovy, 1699, from Mr. John Deane, son of Sir Anthony, master-shipwright there.]

[This is entered as a title in the index, but does not appear in the volume itself, which has only 958 numbered pages.]

Contents of my XI Volumes of Miscellanies, Political, Historical, and Naval.

Paper, folio.   pp. 114.   Marbled boards with gilt tooled leather back and red label to match the volumes of *Miscellanies*.

This volume contains the tables of contents of the eleven volumes of *Miscellanies* re-copied.   **[2880.]**

[An 'Index of such matters as have not been copied out of Mr. Pepys his Manuscripts' of *Miscellanea*, in eleven volumes, is in B.M. Add. MSS. 30221.]

The Journal of Captain James Jenifer on board the Saudades in her voyage from London to Lisbon and back, 12 October 1672 to 1 June 1673.

Paper, folio.   pp. 92 unpaged, many blank.   Vellum, with thin sheepskin back ; with portfolio fastenings.

Contents.   The volume is dedicated to the King.   The journal of the voyage is illustrated by sketches and diagrams, but the greater part of the book contains an account of Lisbon—religion, laws, 'their behaviours and customs,' buildings, fortifications, commodities, provisions, 'the country,' 'the prince,' 'his navy,' etc., the rivers of Lisbon, and 'the present state of Portugal,' with lists of English factors and merchants trading there.   **[2894.]**

[The Saudades was the Queen's ship, and Captain Jenifer was in her special service. (See *Catalogue of Pepysian MSS.* ii 409*n*).]

Bolland's Mediterranean Journal . . . .

Paper, folio. pp. 12 unpaged + 68. Standard binding, but with panel.

Contents. 'Descriptions and Draughts relating to several Ports, Moles, and Currents in the Mediterranean : presented to Mr. Pepys, Secretary of the Admiralty of England, by the said Captain Richard Bolland, one of the Officers of the Mole at Tangier, 1676.' The coloured maps and drawings, as also the text, are on two thicknesses of paper or thin pasteboard. Bolland's original letter of dedication to Pepys is pasted into the beginning of the book.   **[2899.]**

[The first part of this Journal, containing 'A Draught of the Strait's Mouth at Gibraltar' and 'A Description of the Sounding-Boat for Currents,' is printed in Churchill's *Voyages*, iv. 782-end. A full account of the Mole at Tangier is given in Routh, *Tangier*, pp. 343–64.]

S.P.'s Day Collection.

Paper, folio. pp. 3 index + pp. 92, the last 5 pp. being blank. Marbled paper covers ; gilt edges ; the whole inserted in a dark green morocco portfolio, with crown in gilt, and red label ' 1684.'   **[2902]**

Contents. A selection of papers in constant use by Pepys during his second secretaryship, 1684–88 ; most of them occur elsewhere in the Collection. The following is a full list :

P. 1.—10 June, 1684. Letters patents for the erecting the office of secretary of the admiralty of England and creating Samuel Pepys Esq. first secretary therein.

 [See *Catalogue of Pepysian MSS.* i. 65. Other copies are in MS. No. 2867 (*Naval Precedents,* p. 39 *q.v.*), and in *Admiralty Letters,* x. 1.]

P. 3.—A general list of the royal navy as the same was . . . reported to Mr. Pepys by the principal officers and commissioners of the navy at his return to the secretaryship of the admiralty, May, 1684.

P. 10.—The duty of the Lord High Admiral of England first ascertained and declared by the King in council [13 June, 1673].

 [See *Catalogue of Pepysian MSS.* i. 36. *Cf.* also MS. No. 2867 (*Naval Precedents,* p. 35); MS. No. 2870 (*Miscellanies* ii. 401); and S.P. Dom. Car. II. cccxxxv. 303.]

P. 13.—His Majesty's establishment of the number, qualifications, and duties of volunteers and midshipmen extraordinary [8 May, 1676].

[See *Catalogue of Pepysian MSS.* vol. iii. p. xxx. *Cf.* also MS. No. 2867 (*Naval Precedents,* p. 156).]

P. 17.—The qualifications established by his Majesty and the lords of the admiralty, 18 Dec., 1677, without which no person is to be thenceforth held capable of the employment of a lieutenant in any of his Majesty's ships.

[*Cf. Catalogue of Pepysian MSS.* i. 203. Quoted in MS. No. 2867 (*Naval Precedents,* p. 241).]

P. 19.—Resolutions taken by his Majesty for the better regulating the choice of chaplains for the future service of his ships at sea [15 Dec., 1677].

[Discussed in *Catalogue of Pepysian MSS.* i. 206. Another copy is in MS. No. 2867 (*Naval Precedents,* p. 161).]

P. 21.—The establishment of wages to the several flags during the present war [26 Feb.], 1665-6.

[Noted in *Catalogue of Pepysian MSS.* i. 140. *Cf.* also MS. No. 2867 (*Naval Precedents,* p. 217).]

P. 22.—Establishment of pensions to flag-officers serving in his Majesty's first war with Holland [17 July, 1668].

[Summarised in *Catalogue of Pepysian MSS.* i. 145. Another copy is in MS. 2867 (*Naval Precedents,* p. 477).]

P. 23.—Establishment of rewards to officers wounded in fight [6 June, 1673].

[Summarised in *Catalogue of Pepysian MSS.* i. 148. Other copies are in MS. No. 2874 (*Miscellanies* vi. 67) and in MS. No. 2867 (*Naval Precedents,* p. 218).]

P. 24.—An explanatory establishment of rewards for wounds in the case of flag-officers [27 March, 1674].

[Noted in *Catalogue of Pepysian MSS.* i. 149n. Other copies are in MS. No. 2867 (*Naval Precedents,* p. 221) and in MS. No. 2874 (*Miscellanies* vi. 69).]

P. 25.—An establishment of half-pay to be allowed in intervals of employment during peace to commanders of 1st and 2nd rates and 2nd captains of flagships employed in war [6 May, 1674].

[Summarised in *Catalogue of Pepysian MSS.* i. 146. Another copy is in MS. No. 2867 (*Naval Precedents,* p. 164); see also *ib.* p. 259.]

P. 27.—An establishment of pensions to flag-officers serving in his Majesty's second war with Holland [26 June, 1674].

[Noted in *Catalogue of Pepysian MSS.* i. 145. Another copy is in MS. No. 2867 (*Naval Precedents,* p. 222).]

P. 28.—A supplemental establishment of pensions to commanders-in-chief of a limited number of ships of war, [19 May], 1675.

[Summarised in *Catalogue of Pepysian MSS.* i. 147. Another copy is in MS. No. 2867 (*Naval Precedents,* p. 165).]

P. 29.—An establishment of half-pay to be allowed in intervals of employment during peace to masters of 1st and 2nd rate ships employed within the last war, [19 May], 1675.

[Summarised in *Catalogue of Pepysian MSS.* i. 147. Another copy is in MS. No. 2867 (*Naval Precedents,* p. 167); see also *ib.* p. 261.]

F

P. 30.—A regulation first proposed by the lords of the admiralty to the officers of the navy touching cabins, [30 July], 1673.
[The establishment is printed in *Catalogue of Pepysian MSS.* i. 189-92. *Cf.* also MS. No. 2867 (*Naval Precedents,* p. 525).]

P. 31.—The report of the officers of the navy upon the regulation proposed to be established in the business of cabins, [15 Aug., 1673].
[The establishment is printed in *Catalogue of Pepysian MSS.* i. 189-192. *Cf.* also MS. No. 2867 (*Naval Precedents,* p. 525).]

P. 34.—A confirmation of the foregoing report touching cabins [16 Oct., 1673].
[See *Catalogue of Pepysian MSS.* i. 189.]

P. 35.—His Royal Highness James, Duke of York, his commission as Lord High Admiral of England, Ireland, and Wales, etc. [29 Jan., 12 Car. II].
[*Latin.*]
[Another copy is in MS. No. 2870 (*Miscellanies* ii. 389).]

P. 46.—His Majesty's letters patents constituting Prince Rupert, etc., his commissioners for executing the office of Lord High Admiral of England upon the Duke's surrendry thereof, [9 July], 1673.
[See *Catalogue of Pepysian MSS.* i. 38. Other copies are in MS. No. 2867 (*Naval Precedents,* p. 144), and MS. No. 2870 (*Miscellanies* ii. 405.]

P. 50.—His Majesty's letters patents constituting Sir Henry Capel etc. his commissioners for executing the office of Lord High Admiral of England, [14 May], 1679.
[Noted in *Catalogue of Pepysian MSS.* i. 57-8. Other copies are in MS. No. 2867 (*Naval Precedents,* p. 236) and MS. No. 2870 (*Miscellanies* ii. 413).]

P. 54.—His Majesty's letters patents determining the preceding commission for executing the office of Lord High Admiral of England, [19 May], 1684.
[See *Catalogue of Pepysian MSS.* i. 65. Another copy is in MS. No. 2867 (*Naval Precedents,* p. 169).]

P. 55.—The commissioners of admiralty, their solemn act of retrenchment of the charge of the navy by letter to the officers thereof, [29] Dec., 1679.
[Discussed in *Catalogue of Pepysian MSS.* i. 62. Another copy is in MS. No. 2867 (*Naval Precedents,* p. 174).]

P. 59.—An establishment of the numbers of men and of the numbers and natures of the guns fit to be made and confirmed upon every of his Majesty's ships . . . . [confirmed 3 Nov., 1677].
[See *Catalogue of Pepysian MSS.* i. 233. *Cf.* also MS. No. 1340, and MS. No. 2867 (*Naval Precedents,* p. 202).]

P. 64.—An establishment of the number of men and guns to be allowed to the ships . . . built . . . since the aforegoing general establishment . . . . . [31 Oct., 1684].
[See *Catalogue of Pepysian MSS.* i. 236 and MS. No. 2867 (*Naval Precedents,* p. 205).]

P. 65.—An establishment of relief for superannuated officers, [6 Dec.], 1672.
[Summarised in *Catalogue of Pepysian MSS.* i. 148. Another copy is in MS. No. 2867 (*Naval Precedents,* p. 198).]

P. 67.—An establishment of gratuities to the wives, orphans, and kindred of persons slain in his Majesty's service at sea, [17 Jan.], 1672-3.
[See *Catalogue of Pepysian MSS.* i. 134. *Cf.* also MS. No. 2874 (*Miscellanies* vi. 47) and MS. No. 2867 (*Naval Precedents,* pp. 335-43).]

P. 70.—25 Jan., 1684–5. An abstract of the rules about the flag and topsail, and salutes by guns, at this day established and observed by the King's ships, at home and abroad, with respect to those of foreign princes.
[Another copy is in MS. No. 2877 (*Miscellanies* ix. 305).]

P. 72.—The general reduction of the ordinary, and standing establishment made therein, 29 Jan., 1684–5.

P. 74.—A proclamation for regulating the colours to be worn on merchants' ships [18 Sept., 1674].
[A printed copy is in MS. No. 2877 (*Miscellanies* ix. 437).]

P. 75.—The establishment about cripples, 6 May, 1674.

P. 76.—An account of the ships annually employed in the herring, Turkey, Newfoundland, Iceland, Italian, and Canary convoys in and since the year 1680.

P. 78.—An account of the disposal of all his Majesty's ships and vessels employed in sea-pay at Mr. Pepys's return to the secretaryship of the admiralty, May, 1684.

P. 79.—An abstract of the victualling declarations, and annual distributions thereof to the distinct victualling ports, from 1673 to 1686.

P. 80.—A table of the number of commission, warrant, and ordinary officers allowed by the practice of his Majesty's navy to a ship of each rate; with their respective monthly and annual wages. Given me, November 1684, by Sir Richard Haddock, comptroller thereof, as the rule of his paying off the same.

P. 81.—26 Jan., 1685–6. Mr. Pepys's proposition upon the subject of his late general report of the ill state of the navy [with the letter thereon of the special commission to the King, dated 30 March, 1686].
[See *Catalogue of Pepysian MSS.* i. 69-72. *Cf.* also MS. No. 1490.]

P. 83.—Volunteers and officers of land-forces at sea to be treated in the case of wounds, widows, and orphans, as sea-officers are [15 Oct., 1673].
[See *Catalogue of Pepysian MSS.* i. 149. *Cf.* also MS. No. 2867 (*Naval Precedents*, p. 219).]

P. 84.—15 July, 1686. His Majesty's regulation in the business of plate carriage, etc., with his establishment of an allowance for their tables, and other encouragements to his sea-commanders.
[Discussed in *Catalogue of Pepysian MSS.* i. 210. Another copy is in MS. No. 2867 (*Naval Precedents*, p. 245), and the establishment is printed in Pepys's *Memoirs relating to the State of the Royal Navy*, pp. 102-126.]

Sir Anthony Deane's Doctrine of Naval Architecture . . . .

Paper, folio. 2 pp. blank + folded table of contents inset + 42 folded sheets of text, drawings of ships, and tables inset, paged as 1–86, + 13 engravings of ships. Standard binding.

Contents. "Doctrine of naval architecture and tables of dimensions, materials, furniture, and expense appertaining thereto; written in the year 1670, at the instance of Samuel Pepys, Esq. . . . . with a set of naval prints engraved by R. Zeeman, published by Arthur Tooker, and

dedicated to Mr. Pepys.   Anno. 1675." These are delicate and elaborate
pen-and-ink drawings of a ship of each rate.   **[2910.]**

['Mr. Pepys, late Secretary to the Admiralty, showed me a large folio containing the
whole mechanic part and art of building royal ships and men of war, made by Sir Anthony
Deane, being so accurate a piece from the very keel to the lead block, rigging, guns,
victualling, manning, and even to every individual pin and nail, in a method so astonish-
ing and curious, with a draught, both geometiical and in perspective, and several
sections, that I do not think the world can show the like.   I esteem this book as an
extraordinary jewel.'   Evelyn's *Diary*, 28 Jan. 1682.]

Miscellaneous Naval Manuscripts.

   Paper, folio.   pp. 206 unpaged, some blank. *Temp.* Jac. I.   Standard
binding.

   Contents. (1) A list of ships [*temp.* Jac. I]. (2) 'A proportion for the
rigging of all these ships following,' 1611. (3) 'A true length of all the
masts and yards of the ships undernamed, taken in anno 1600.'
(4) 'Rules for measuring of masts of all sorts,' November, 1590.
(5) Prices of masts. (6) 'Instructions drawn by Sir John Trevor, Kt.,
in anno 1603, for the ordering of receipts and issues of provisions
for his Majesty's Navy.'   (7) Various instructions to the officials at
Chatham, 1604–6.   (8) Copies of various letters and warrants, 1604–9.
(9) Surveys made in 1611 of the following ships:

Elizabeth Jonas	Warspite	Antelope	Advantagia
Prince	Assurance	Dreadnought	Gallaryta
Triumph	Vanguard	Speedwell	Volatilia
Bear	Red Lion	Adventure	Crane
Merehonora	Nonsuch	Advantage	Quittance
Ann Royal	Maryrose	Tremontane	Charles
Repulse	Defiance	Spy	
Garland	Rainbow	Primrose	

                                                       [2911.]

Collection of Vessels Naval.

   Vellum, oblong, 17¾ × 13¼.   5 pp. paper blank + 1 p. paper
contents + ff. 1–32 vellum + pp. 33–41 paper + 1 p. paper blank.
Temp. Car. II.   Standard binding, but with panel.

   Contents. F. 1, 'Mr. Dummer's Draughts of the Body of an English
Man of War.'   Delicate sepia drawings.
[*Cf.* MS. No. 1074 and note.]
F. 33, 'Mr. Nichols's Draught of the Double Canoe found by Schouten

in the South Seas ; from the Description and Print thereof in my Latin edition of his Voyages, No. 677, B. 243.' Drawing in colour.

[No. 677, B. 243, is the old shelf mark—now No. 1045. The print from which the drawing is made is inserted opposite p. 29 of Schouten's work, and there is inserted at the end 'A transcript of so much of the original Dutch edition of Schouten's *Voyage into the South Sea* as relates to the double-bottom vessels or double canoes there first by him discovered about the Isle of Cocos, and the account given of them in his journal' of 9–13 May, 1616.]

F. 34, 'Mr. Hunt's two Draughts in perspective of Sir William Petty's Double Bottom.' Drawings in colour.

[An account of Sir William Petty's experiment is given in MS. No. 2874 (*Miscellanies* vi. 1).]

F. 36, 'Mr. Nichols's Draught of Captain Dampier's Ladrone-Boat, from its model built by Mr. Phillips, an officer of the Navy.' Drawing in colour.

F. 37, 'Mr. Nichols's Draught of Mr. Phillips's own drawing, laid down geometrically, and presented to me by himself.' Drawing in colour.

F. 39, 'Mr. Nichols's draught of a Bantam-Proe, from the model provided and presented to me by my honoured friend Sir James Houblon.' Drawing in colour.

F. 41, 'Captain Thomas Phillips's Draughts of a portable vessel of wicker, ordinarily used by the wild Irish.' Sepia drawings. **[2934.]**

[Probably Thomas Phillips, the engineer. See *D.N.B.* xlv. 214.]

A Register of the Ships of the Royal Navy of England from the Restoration of King Charles II, May, 1660, to the day of King James II his withdrawing and the determination of Mr. Pepys's relation thereto, December 18, 1688.

Paper, folio. pp. 8 unpaged + 110. Standard binding ; gilt edges. **[2940.]**

[This register is printed in *Catalogue of Pepysian MSS.* i. 253–306 (*N.R.S.* Publications, vol. xxvi). Similar registers from Pepys's collection are in Bodl. Rawlinson MSS. A. 197.]

Sea Commission Officers, My Naval Register . . . between the Restoration of King Charles II, May, 1660, and the withdrawing of . . . King James II, December, 1688.

Paper, folio. pp. 16 unpaged + 128. Standard binding ; gilt edges. **[2941.]**

[This register is printed in *Catalogue of Pepysian MSS.* i. 307–435 (*N.R.S.* Publications, vol. xxvi). A similar register from Pepys's collection is in Bodl. Rawlinson MSS. A. 199 ; see also A. 181, f. 197 and A. 186, f. 141.]

A Set of Sea-Charts, specially prepared towards the strict adjustment of the Lengths of the several Coasting Lines of England, Scotland, Ireland, France, United Provinces and the Danish round Jutland, Spain.

Paper (two thicknesses), large folio, 21 × 15.   ff. 24, paged 1–6. Art boards ; leather back.

Prints of ships, dolphins, and symbolic figures, cut out and coloured, are pasted on to the maps.   **[2970.]**

A Declaration of the Royal Navy of England, composed by Anthony Anthony, one of the Officers of the Ordnance, and by him presented to King Henry VIII, Anno Regni 38°, Domini 1546, in three parchment rolls (here thus reduced) containing, viz. : Roll 1st, Ships, 2nd, Galliasses, 3rd, Pinnaces and Row-barges, whereof the 1st and 3rd were given me anno 1680 by my Royal Master King Charles II, and the other (since found) is resting, anno 1690, in the Royal Library at St. James's.

The original rolls containing coloured drawings of the ships are cut and pieced so as to make a large parchment folio volume.   Ff. 6 unpaged + ff. 100 paged.   Red morocco, with panels elaborately tooled in gilt (probably by Mearne) ; silver-gilt clasps, bearing the arms, crest, and monogram of Samuel Pepys ; gilt edges.

Ff. 45-48 consist of two thicknesses of pasteboard inserted after the 1st roll, containing " A General Abstract of the Equipage and Furniture of the Ships of the preceding Roll." F. 51 gives an abstract of the contents of the absent 2nd Roll [now in the British Museum, Add. MSS. 22047]. F. 100, A list of the Royal Navy of England, anno 1546, contained in the three Rolls, with a note " that the Galliasse part of the foregoing abstract and draughts is taken from the original Roll thereof resting in the King's Library at St. James's, lent me by my friend Mr. Thynne, Library-keeper there, as the other two are from the original Rolls in my own hands, given me by my royal master King Charles II." A figure of Henry VIII, cut out of a print, is pasted into the end of the volume.   **[2991.]**

[The drawings in these rolls may in all probability be accepted as an authoritative record of the general features of the hull of a given type of craft ; although, as there is a tendency to depict the same type again and again, it would not be safe to conclude that they really represent the hulls of particular ships. As regards the rigging the value of the drawings is much less.   Omissions are numerous, and there is much that would be unworkable in a real ship.   Although the artist evidently understands the meaning of much that he draws, he does not display complete seaman's knowledge.   Artists who are not seamen, when they represent ships, as a rule deal more accurately with the hull, which is a kind of building, than with the rigging, which is a complex and unfamiliar piece of machinery. A list of the ships, with particulars of their equipment, is printed in Derrick, *Memoirs of the Royal Navy*, pp. 303–7. An engraving of the Harry Grace à Dieu is in Charnock, *Marine Architecture*, ii. 32, and photographic reproductions of the Murrian and the Struse are in E. Keble Chatterton, *Sailing Ships*, facing p. 188. MS. No. 2219 (q.v. *supra*) is an abstract of these rolls, with copies of some of the illuminations on a reduced scale, probably made for Pepys before the original rolls came into his possession].

A State of the Shores on each side of the Thames between London Bridge and Cuckold's Point, arising from a Double Survey thereof in the years 1684 and 1687.

Large paper folio, 24 × 14. ff. 38, some blank; maps paged 1–22. Standard binding, but with panel; gilt edges.

Contents. (1) A survey of the buildings and encroachments on the river of Thames, on both sides, from London Bridge eastward to the lower end of Limehouse, taken by the Principal Officers and Commissioners of his Majesty's Navy, with the assistance of the Elder Brethren of Trinity House, in pursuance of an order of the Right Hon. the Lords Commissioners for executing the office of Lord High Admiral of England, dated 1 March, 1683–4 . . . .

[The survey itself is dated 30 October, 1684.]

(2) A survey of the river of Thames on each side (in six sheets) from London Bridge downward to Cuckold's Point and Limehouse, expressing the present state of the same . . . by the Principal Officers and Commissioners of the Navy (assisted by the Corporation of the Trinity House . . .) A.D. 1686; and presented to his Majesty by the said Principal Officers and Commissioners with their Report thereon, dated 21 July, 1687. [2997.]

[The six maps of the Thames are signed by the Principal Officers and by the Elder Brethren of the Trinity House.]

END OF THE "SEA" MSS.

INDEX

[*⁎* *Where reference is made to a separate work, the title is printed in italics.*]

Abuses in the navy :   PAGE

    Lord Burghley's memorial against abuses ... ...   54 (p. 632)
    form of commission authorising enquiry into, since 1579... ...   51 (p. 145)
    certain articles ... against John Hawkyns, ... 1587   51
    a letter concerning Sir Robert Mansell's demands of imprest money,
       ... 1620   43
    complaints by John Hollond, paymaster of the navy, 1636...   52 (pp. 270, 273)
    Sir William Monson's paper of propositions ... 1636   52
    several representations ... of the ill state of ... the navy, 1659–60 ...   12
    notes by Pepys on abuses in the navy, 1664–72 ... ... 18 (No. 2581)
    miscellaneous papers relating to abuses   59–61
  See also " Commissions."
Adams, Clement   5
Admirals :
    instructions—
      by Lord Clinton, 1548   2
      by William Wynter, 1558   2
      by George, Marquis of Buckingham   19
      by Popham, Blake, and Deane ... to sea-commanders, 1650 ...   61
      by the ... admirals of the fleet during the late rebellion, with
        additions by Sir William Penn   20
    lists of, from 1307 to 1660   44
            from 48 Henr. III to 27 Eliz.   53
  See also " Lord High Admiral."
Admiralty :
    admiral of Scotland, commission granted by, 1672   48
    advocates, list of, since 1660   44
    affairs of the admiralty, papers relating to 27, 44
    Black Book of the Admiralty—
      abstract of   44
      transcript of   44
      inquisition at Queenborough, 1375   42

G

Admiralty—*continued.*   PAGE

     ordinances ... of Edward III   42
     ordinance of King John at Hastings   42
     Lorrain's translation of the three foregoing documents   42
   commissions of ... *see* " Commissions."
   court of—
     fees to officials of the ...   44
     instructions for the Dutch ... 1597   7
     proceedings in the ...   2, 44
     the charges attending the same   44
   establishment of the ... by Charles II, 1660 ...   20
   instructions for the ... 1647   20
   judges of the ... 5 Henr. VIII to 1685   44
   jurisdiction of the ...   7
   office of the ... in the reign of Charles I   20
   persons employed in the ... 1687   22
   secretaries of the ... 1660–88   27
   statutes and ordinances for ... under-officers of the ...   49
Admiralty Journal, 1674–9   26
Admiralty Letters, 1673–9, 1684–9 ...   25
Admiralty Library, duplicates of Pepysian MSS. in ...   viii
Admiralty Precedents ...   27
Algiers :
   corsairs at, 1685   53
   force by sea at, 1687   31, 61
   French proceedings at, 1682–3 ...   47, 53
   men-of-war at, 1685   50
   reprisals against, 1680, 1681   37(2), 38
   shipbuilding at, 1680   46
Amazon, description of the ...   47
America :
   intended history of ...   47
   plantations in   47
Amsterdam, state of shipping at, 1686   62
Anthony Anthony's *Declaration of the Royal Navy* ...   70
     abstract of the *Declaration* ...   10
Appointments* (by commission, patent, warrant, etc.) :
   Anglesey, Earl of, a commissioner of the admiralty, 1673   29
   Arlington, Earl of, a commissioner of the admiralty, 1673   29
   Beach, Sir Richard, a commissioner of the navy, 1686 ...   28, 29
   Bedford, Mr. Thomas, register of the admiralty (in reversion), 1685 ...   33, 49

---

* *cf.* Bodl., Rawlinson MSS. A 216 (" copies of royal commissions, appointments, and orders in Council issued in the reigns of Charles I and Charles II ... concerning the navy ...").

Appointments—*continued.*   PAGE
Berkeley, Lord, a commissioner of the navy, 1660   34
Berry, Sir John, a commissioner of the navy, 1686   ...   .28(2), 29
Bowler, John, register of the vice-admiralty in the ... Isle of Wight, 1685   49
Buckingham, Duke of, a commissioner of the admiralty, 1673   29
Bullock, Mr. John, chief chyrurgeon at Dover, 1672   36
Capel, Sir Henry, a commissioner of the admiralty, 1679...   ... 32, 40, 41, 66
Carteret, Sir George, treasurer of the navy, 1660   34
   „   „   a commissioner of the admiralty, 1673   29
Coventry, Henry, Esq., a commissioner of the admiralty, 1673   ...   29
Deane, Sir Anthony, a commissioner of the navy, 1686 ...   .28(2), 29
Falkland, Lord, treasurer of the navy, 1681   62
Fauconberg, Henry, LL.D., judge of the vice-admiralty ot Norfolk,
   1681   49
Fenn, Nicholas, Esq., a commissioner for victualling, 1683   28
Finch, Daniel, Esq., a commissioner of the admiralty, 1679   32
Franklin (or Franckyn), Samuel, Esq., procurator in maritime and
   ecclesiastical causes, 1673 and 1685   ...   .   33, 37
Gauden, Jonathan, Esq., agent-general and muster-master at
   Gibraltar, 1685   30
Gill, John, marshal in South Cornwall, 1683   49
Godwin, Sir John, a commissioner of the navy, 1686   ...   .28(2), 29
Grafton, Henry, Duke of, vice-admiral and lieutenant-general of the
   admiralty of England, 1683 ...   . 28, 49
Haddock, Sir Richard, a commissioner for victualling, 1683   28
   „   „   a commissioner of the navy, 1686   ...   ...28(2), 29
Hales, Edward, Esq., a commissioner of the admiralty, 1679   32
Herbert, Arthur, Esq., rear-admiral of England, 1684, 1685 ...   ...28, 49(2)
Hewer, Mr. William, a commissioner of the navy, 1686 ...   .28(2), 29
Holmes, Sir Robert, continued as vice-admiral of Hampshire, 1685 ...   ' 33
Jenkins, Sir Leoline, judge of the admiralty, 1685   ...   .   49(2)
Joynes, Mr. William, continued as marshal of the admiralty, 1685   ...   33, 49
Kent, Earl of, lord high admiral, 1461   42
Lauderdale, Duke of, a commissioner of the admiralty, 1673   29
Lee, Sir Thomas, a commissioner of the admiralty, 1679   32
Lindsey, Robert, Earl of, a commissioner of the admiralty, 1635   ... 48, 49
   „   „   „   admiral...of a particular fleet ... 1635   ...   48
Lloyd, Sir Richard, advocate-general, 1685   49
Mennes, Sir John, vice-admiral in the narrow seas, 1661   43
Meres, Sir Thomas, a commissioner of the admiralty, 1679   32
Monmouth, Duke of, a commissioner of the admiralty, 1673   29
Narbrough, Sir John, a commissioner of the navy, 1686 ...   .28(2), 29
Northumberland, Algernon, Earl of, admiral of a particular fleet,
   1636, 1637 ...   .   48(2)

Appointments—*continued.*   PAGE

Northumberland, Algernon, Earl of, lord high admiral, 1638   49
Oldys, William, LL.D., advocate-general, 1686   37
Ormonde, Duke of, a commissioner of the admiralty, 1673   29
Osborne, Viscount, a commissioner of the admiralty, 1673   29
Parsons, John, Esq., a commissioner for victualling, 1683   28
Pearse, James, Esq., chyrurgeon-general of the navy, 1686   32
Penn, Sir William, a commissioner of the navy, 1660   34
Pepys, Samuel, Esq., secretary of the admiralty, 1684 ...   . 27, 64
Pett, Peter, Esq., a commissioner of the navy, 1660   34
Pett, Sir Phineas, a commissioner of the navy, 1686   ...   .28(2), 29
Pinfold, Dr. Thomas, advocate-general, 1685   32
Porter, Charles, Esq., counsel for the navy, 1685   32
Raines, Sir Richard, judge of the admiralty, 1686   32
Rupert, Prince, vice-admiral of England, 1672   29
„   „   a commissioner of the admiralty, 1673 ...   ...   29, 40, 66
St. Michel, Balthazar, Esq., a commissioner of the navy, 1686   ...   28, 29
Sandwich, Earl of, vice-admiral of the navy and admiral of the narrow
  seas, 1660   29
Sandwich, Earl of, admiral in the narrow seas, 1661   ...   .   42(2)
„   „   admiral for the then expedition, 1661   42
Seymour, Edward, Esq., a commissioner of the admiralty, 1673   ...   29
„   „   treasurer of the navy, 1673   62
Shaftesbury, Earl of, a commissioner of the admiralty, 1673   29
Sotherne, James, Esq., a commissioner of the navy, 1686   ...   ...28(2), 29
Stiles, Henry, LL.D., judge of the admiralty of Ireland, 1685   ...   49
Sturt, Anthony, Esq., a commissioner for victualling, 1683   28
Tippetts, Sir John, a commissioner of the navy, 1686 ...   .28(2), 29
Tredenham, Sir Joseph, vice-admiral of North Cornwall, 1679   49
Vaughan, Edward, Esq., a commissioner of the admiralty, 1679   ...   32
Watkinson, Dr., continued as judge of the vice-admiralty of Hamp-
  shire... 1685   33
Weston, Lord, a commissioner of the admiralty, 1628 and 1632   ... 47, 48
Winch, Sir Humphrey, a commissioner of the admiralty, 1679   ...   32
Yard, Robert, Esq., muster-master in the narrow seas, 1683   33
York, James, Duke of, lord high admiral, 1661 ...   . 40, 66
forms of appointment, certificate, or licence   ...   .   38(4)
„   commission, patent, or warrant   ...   .37(8), 38
See also " Commissions."
Archdeacon, Daniel   45
Army :
  charge of the army prepared against the Spaniards, 1587-8   54
  discourse of the army... in the haven of Lisbon, 1588   45
  project ... for defence against a landing of any army...   ...   ... 7, 42
See also " Land-forces," " Land-militia."

Baker, Christopher : PAGE
  complaints against 59
  his proposals for reformation of the navy 60
Balfour's *Practiques* 10
Baptisings, marriages, and burials, a more perfect register of 40
Battine, Edward, *Method of Building ... Ships of War* 1
Bedford, Mr. Thomas :
  appointed register of the admiralty (in reversion), 1685 ... ... 33, 49
  his commonplace book 43
  his letter to Pepys, 1678 7
  references to authors upon the flag, 1685 55
  translations by 44
Beverland, Adrian, of Middelburg 7
Blake, Robert, admiral 61
Bolland's *Mediterranean Journal* 64
Boreman, Sir William, his hospital at Greenwich 50
Bowles, Mr. Phineas, secretary of the admiralty ... ... 63(2)
Brook House, commissioners of accounts at 50
Buck, Peter, clerk of the navy :
  his complaints of abuses ... ... 60(4)
Buck, Thomas :
  his complaints of abuses ... ... 60(2)
Buckingham, George, Marquis of :
  his instructions for the government of the navy 19
Burghley, Lord :
  on abuses in the navy 54
  on "public matters, and chiefly Spain" 54
  references to 3, 7, 42
Button, Sir Thomas :
  a report touching his accounts, 1618–9 43
Byam, Lieut.-General William :
  his narrative of the state of Guiana ... 1665 47

Cabins, establishment of, 1673 ... ... 36, 66(3)
Cæsar, Sir Julius, transcripts from his library 39
Captains' tables, establishment for, 1686 ... ... 32, 67
Carew, George, Esq. :
  considerations relating to trade, by ... 1684 47
Carteret, Sir George, treasurer of the navy 29, 34, 50
Castle, Mr., contract with, 1670 12
Chaplains, regulations for the choice of, 1677 ... ... 30, 65
  „   „   „   alteration in, 1687 30

Charles II :   PAGE
   dedications to   ...   .   19(2)
   references to 20, 58, 70
Chatham :
   abuses at   ...   .   59(2)
   Chest at—
      abstract of the account of, 1617–37   52
      orders concerning payments to, 1668 and 1688   ...   .35, 38(2)
      standing rules of relief from the, 1685   48
   commissioner at, 1686   ...   .   28, 29
   harbour at   32
   instructions to officials at, 1604–5   68
   the King's visit to, 1688   62
   survey of ships at, 1624   52
Christ's Hospital 9, 58
Chyrurgeons, appointment of   ...   .   38(2)
Cinque Ports, the :
   arms of   6
   ships belonging to 51, 53
   wardens of   6
Clerk of the navy, antiquity of the office of   61
Clinton, Lord, admiral of the fleet :
   articles appointed by, 1548   2
Commissions :
   of admiralty, 1628, appointment of   47
      ,,   1632   ,,   ,, ...   48
      ,,   1635   ,,   ,, ...   48
      ,,   1673   ,,   ,, ...   29, 40, 66
      ,,   ,, minutes of   26
      ,,   1679, appointment of   ...   .   40, 41(2), 66
      ,,   ,, criticism of, by Pepys   4
      ,,   ,, determined, 1684   ...   .   30, 66
   of enquiry, 1608, examination of witnesses by   60
      ,,   ,, report of   ...   .   8, 42 (p. 355)
      ,,   1618   ,, ...   21
   special commission of 1686, appointment of   ...   .   28(6), 29(5)
      ,,   ,,   ,, S.P.'s diary relating to   ...   .   ii, 4
      ,,   ,,   ,, report of first year's proceedings of   ...   23
      ,,   ,,   ,,   ,, second   ,,   ,,   ...   24
   to Sir Francis Drake and others to provide against an invasion from
      Spain, 1595   51
   to the Bishop of London and others, 1636   48
   for letters of marque, 1665   37
   for prizes, 1665   37

Commissions—*continued.*   PAGE
    for sick and wounded, 1672 ... ... 36(2)
    for widows and orphans, 1673 and 1674 ... ...33, 34 (p. 342)
    for victualling, 1683 28
    forms of commission 32
Commonplace-book of Mr. Bedford, register of the admiralty 43
Commons, House of ... .14(3), 45
  See also " Parliament."
Convoy :
    account of ships employed in 30, 67
    instructions to ... . 33(7)
    proposal for 42
    representation of the merchants concerning, 1676? 30
Cook-rooms, a discourse concerning, 1618 42
Cordage :
    objections against Mr. Wells's proposal 18
    a proposition shewing how England might be the staple for cordage... 51
    a proposition for preserving ... cordage 53
Cotton, Sir Robert :
    letter in behalf of Sir John Trevor ... 1608 60
    letters to ... . 60(2)
    Library 38
    on the discipline of the navy 54
Council-books, extracts from, 1541–53 9
Court-martial, Sir Richard Raines's opinion concerning, 1688? 38
Coventry, Sir William :
    his proposal for reducing the charge of the navy, 1667 13
    references to 20, 22
Cowley, William Ambrosia, mariner :
    his voyage round the globe, 1683–6 24
Cripples, establishment for, 1674 67

Dartmouth, Lord :
    remarks upon a project for victualling, 1673 43
    instructions to the commanders at Tangier, 1684 33
    dedication to, 1685 1
Dean, Forest of :
    state of, 1671 12
Deane, Sir Anthony :
    Method of measuring ... a Ship 16
    Doctrine of Naval Architecture ... , 1670 67
    observations on the state of the fleet, 1674 45
    Collections touching the ... Navy of France ... 1675 10
    observations upon the improvement of our frigates in sailing, 1675 ... 46

Deane, Sir Anthony—*continued.* PAGE
    on the proportion of able seamen to ordinary 14
    report about shipwrights, 1675 13
    memorandum about galley-frigates, 1676 46
    appointed a commissioner of the navy, 1686 ... ...28(2), 29
    minutes of the King's visit to Chatham, 1688 62
Deane, Mr. John :
    letter about galley-frigates, 1676 46
    on the naval forces of Muscovy, 1699 63
De Gerente, Anthony (alias Clerant) :
    his proposition about ... preserving wood and cordage 53
Deptford :
    ships built at, 1678 ... ... 3(2)
    commissioner at, 1686 ... ... **28**, 29
Discipline :
    the true discipline of the navy ... by Sir Robert Cotton 54
    Ordres des Estats Generaux de Hollande ... 1672 7
Docks :
    in the river of Thames, 1666 43
Dover :
    petition touching the haven at, *c.* 1600 40
    appointment of chief chyrurgeon at, 1672 36
Dover Castle :
    the constables of 6
Drake, Sir Francis, commission to, 1595 51
Dugdale, Sir William :
    catalogus librorum MSS. Musaeo Ashmoleano legatorum a ... 1685–6 .. 62
    correspondence with Pepys i
    form of flags provided by, 1677 56
    reference to 21
Drummers, establishment for beating the English march by ... 1631 50
Dummer, Mr. Edmund :
    draughts of a man-of-war 68
    letter to Pepys about shipbuilding, 1679 2
Dutch :
    admiralty 7
    church in London 62
    East India ships 15
    fleet ... ... 7, 12(2), 13(2), 14, 46(2), 52
    First Dutch War, the—
        merchant-ships hired to serve in 12
        Captain Fowler's discourse ... 1654 27
        Pepys's projected history of i

Dutch—*continued.* PAGE
    Second Dutch War, the—
        accounts of the navy during ... ... 14(3), 17, 19
        merchant-ships hired to serve in 12
        Pepys's defence of the proceedings in 17, 50
        rules for the adjudication of prizes in, 1665 37
    Third Dutch War —
        fleet employed in 1
        ,, ,, ,, abstract of 13
        relations of the battle of 28th May, 1672 45
  See also "Holland."

East India Company 18, 33, 47
Edward III :
    charge of the household of 2
    navy of 45
Edward VI :
    William Thomas's letter to 40
Effingham, Lord Howard of :
    dedication to 22
  See also "Nottingham, Earl of."
Evelyn, Mr. John :
    correspondence with Pepys on naval matters, 1680 45
    references to ... ...i, 36, 39
Exchequer tallies, remarks upon 39

Fenton, Edward :
    his book, 1590 1
    journals of, 1578, 1582–3 8
Finance :
    expenses of the household of Edward III 2
    payments made to the navy ... 1538–41 51
    estimate of the growing charge of a fleet, 1559 2
    estimate of the charge ... against the Spaniards ... 1587–8 54
    financial papers of the early years of James I 39
    expense of the King's household, 1610 40
    an abstract of the account of the Chest at Chatham, 1617–37 52
    a project for contracting the charge of the navy 21, 40
    reports touching accounts, 1618–9, 1620, 1621 ... ...43(2), 51
    estimates of the debt of the navy, 1643–60 ... ... 11(2)
    abstract ,, ,, ,, 1660, 1667, 1672, 1673, 1675 ... 12
    expense of the office of the ordnance, 1660–75 12
    expense of the navy from the beginning of the ... war, ... 1666 ... 19
    papers relating to the accounts of ... 1666 ... ... 14(4)

Finance—*continued.*   PAGE

    Sir William Coventry's proposal for reducing the charge of the navy,
      1667   13

    Naval Accounts, 1667 *and* 1668   18

    order concerning payments to the Chest ... 1668   35

    Mr. Hosier's Method of balancing Storekeepers' Accounts, 1668 ...   6

    abstract of ... prices ... for ... stores, 1668–75   12

    moneys paid for sick and wounded, 1672–3   14

    a state of the debt of the navy, 1672–86   61

    notes of the charge of building 20 ships, 1675?   12

    charge of the navy for 1676   12

    charge of the royal bounty to relations of persons slain at sea ... 1678 14

    calculation of the charge of a naval war, 1678   14

    parallel of the charge of the navy before and after 1679   51

    admiralty commissioners' letter of retrenchment, 1679 ... ...   30, 66

    estimate of the charge of the navy for 1684   34

    charges extraordinary for wages in war   14

    order ... for paying all fines to the Chest ... 1688 ... ...   38(2)

    the Lord Treasurer's virtues in his payments   12

    an estimate of the charge of ... five squadrons   43

Fishery rights :

    Rainsford's project for ... prohibiting strangers to fish ... 1604 39

    papers relating to   59

Five Ports. *See* " Cinque Ports."

Flags :

    a proclamation for regulating ... 1674   67

    an abstract of the rules about ... 1685   67

    Lieutenant Gra[y]don's *Collection of Naval Flags and Colours,* 1686...   5

    an account of divers things concerning the ... right of the flag   44

    the sizes of standards   2

    miscellaneous papers relating to the history of the flag   55–8

Flamsteed, John, first astronomer royal :

    his *Account of ... Navigation,* 1697   8

Foreign posts, table of the   31

Fortree, Mr.   5

Forts and castles along the sea-coasts of England   61

Fowler, Captain :

    his discourse with a Dutch skipper ... 1654   27

France, French :

    King of—

        agreement with, relating to the union of the fleets, 1672 46

        his commission to the Duke of York, 1672   46

          „   „   any commander-in-chief, 1672   46

        ships built by, since 1672   13

France, French—*continued.*   PAGE
    his great works ... at Toulon, etc. ... since 1678 14
    fleet of, navy of ... ... 12(3), 13(4), 14(2), 46(4), 47, 50, 53
    galleys of 46
Freeman, Mr. :
    his bill for preservation ... of timber ... 1675 41

Gibraltar :
    A Discourse touching the Current in the Strait of ... 1675 4
    instructions to the agent-general at ... 1685 30
Gibson, Mr. Richard ... ...16(2), 27
Graving, reasons for, 1627 52
Gra[y]don, Lieutenant John :
    his *Collection of Naval Flags and Colours,* 1686 5
Greaves, Mr. John :
    his papers on navigation, *c.* 1640 9
Green Ribband Club, Journal of, 1678–81 52
Guardships :
    instructions for ... the guardships ... in Chatham and Portsmouth
    harbours, 1685 32
Guiana :
    Byam's narrative of the state of ... 1665 47
Guns :
    establishment of ... men and ... guns, 1677 ... ...3, 31, 66
    ,, ,, ,, ,, ,, 1684 66
    a list of ships with ... guns proposed for each ... 1685 62
    abstract of the aforesaid 62
See also "Ordnance."
Haddock, Sir Richard, comptroller of the navy ... ... 28(3), 29, 30, 45, 67
Hales, Sir Edward :
    proceedings in the case of 62
Halley, Mr. :
    his paper on navigation, 1696 9
Hastings :
    ordinance of King John at 42
    papers relating to the making of a haven at, 1636 52
Hawkyns, Sir John :
    certain articles ... against ... 1587 51
    letters complaining of cheats of ... 1588 ... ... 60, 61
    commission to, 1595 51
Hawkyns, Sir Richard :
    reflections on ... 1608 60
Herring fishery 33, 67

Hewer, Mr. William :   PAGE

    appointed a commissioner of the navy, 1686 ...   .28(2), 29

    his minutes of the King's visit to Chatham, 1688   62

    his account of the secretaries of the admiralty, 1660–88   27

Historians :

    Extracts ... Naval collected out of ... English Historians   21

    A Collection of Extracts Naval out of the Latin-English Historians and

      French   16

Holland :

    list of fleet employed against, 1671–3   1

    preparations making in, 1688   63

    references to   ...   .   7, 24, 48, 56, 65(2)

  See also " Dutch."

Hollond (or Holland), John, paymaster of the navy :

    eight questions by ... 1636   52

    inconveniencies attending payments to wrong parties ... 1636 ...   52

    his *First Discourse of the Navy,* 1638   9

    reasons ... why the master-shipwright should not keep a private yard,

      1652   52

    his *Second Discourse touching the Navy* ... 1659   25

Hollyday, William :

    reasons touching the maintenance of English shipping, 1609   39

Holmes, Sir Robert :

    his journals of two voyages ... 1660–1, 1663–4   20

    continued as vice-admiral of Hampshire ... 1685   33

Hosier, Mr., muster-master at Gravesend :

    his *Method of balancing Storekeepers' Accounts,* 1668   6

Hospitals :

    Sir William Boreman's hospital at Greenwich   50

    marine hospital "designed about Limehouse ..." 1684   50

    a paper relating to the hospital propounded to be built for seamen ...

      1685   50

Houblon, Sir James 62, 69

Humfrey, Jamys :

    The Boke of the Lawe of Olerone   2

Intercursus Magnus, 1496   41

Intrenchment, order of 7, 42

Jamaica :

    considerations concerning ... 1685   47

James I :

    proclamation by, 1606   57

    petition from the Trinity House to ... 1609   39

PAGE

James II :
his *Pocket Book* 1
Jenifer, Captain James :
journal of his voyage to Lisbon, 1672–3 63
letter giving an account of the Spanish West India fleet, 1675 46
Jenkins, Sir Leoline :
his notes about salutes at Livorne, 1681 55
appointed judge of the admiralty, 1685 ... ... 49(2)
Journal, Admiralty, 1674–9 26
Journal of Phineas Pett, 1570–1638 39
See also "Voyages and Journals."
Judge-advocate, the duty of a, 1663 29

Kinsale, Prince Rupert's proceedings at, 1649 38
Kirke, Colonel, Governor of Tangier 40

Land-forces :
officers of, wounded at sea, 1673 ... ... 31, 67
rewards for, 1685 50
Land-militia, a project for a, 1557 ... ... 5, 39
Lepanto, battle of 45
Libellus de Policia Conceruatiua Maris 3
Libro de Cargos 14
Lieutenants :
qualifications and examination of, 1677 ... ... 32, 65
form of the letters ... for ... examinations ... 1687 31
Lisbon :
discourse of the army ... assembled in the haven of ... 1588 45
Captain Jenifer's account of, 1672–3 64
Livorne :
salutes at, 1681 55
victuals at, 1667 18
London, William, lord bishop of :
commission to, 1636 48
London, Mr. William :
his scheme of a history of the plantations, 1680 39
Lord high admiral :
allowances given to, 1622 43
declaration about the future management of the ... office of ... 1687 ... 61
fees of ... [Eliz.] 61
instructions established for ... 1673 ... ... 27, 29, 40, 64
rights of ... ... 44 (p. 291)
„ in time of war, 1666 48

Lord high admiral—*continued.*   PAGE

   sea-whistle worn by 57

   state of the office of, 1628–88 62

Lorrain, Paul :

   his translations from and into French ... ... 42 (p. 233)

Mansell, Sir Robert, treasurer of the navy :

   complaint against ... 1609 60

   his demands of imprest money ... 1620 43

   reports concerning the accounts of, 1620, 1621 ... ... 51, 43

   references to 21, 54, 61

Manwell, Mr. :

   his ... project to keep a registry of seamen ... 1634 52

Marine affairs of England, extracts relating to, 1541–53 9

Mariners :

   a proposal ... for the examining of ... [Eliz.] 54

   the decay of ... 1602 39

Marque and reprisal :

   against Algiers, 1680, 1681 ... ...37(2), 38

   against the Dutch, 1664–5 ... ... 37(4)

Martial laws ... in the time of King Henry VI 41

Martyn, Henry, gentleman :

   his project ... touching a more perfect register of baptisings, marriages,

     and burials 40

Mary (Queen), funeral of, 1695 58

Meadows, Sir Philip :

   his observations touching the dominion ... of the seas 54

Mearne's binding 3, 70

Mediterranean, the :

   Admiral Russell's Expedition to, 1694 15

   Bolland's *Mediterranean Journal* 64

   convoy to ... ... 33(3)

   currents in 64

Men :

   the number of masters, mariners, and fishermen ... 1583 54

   abstract of a certificate ... of ... masters and mariners appertaining to

     the Five Ports, 1587 53

   an account of mariners ... 1590 54

   a list of ... ships ... with ... men, mariners, gunners, and soldiers ...

     1590 54

   abuse of undermanning, 1609 60

   notes about complements [Jac. I] 60

   proposals for lessening the complements ... 1619 42

Men — *continued.* PAGE

mariners, sailors, and fishermen ... within ... South ... Devon, 1619...   7

project to keep a registry of seamen ... 1634   52

lists and establishments shewing the ... numbers of men at several
    times allowed ... 1651–75   47

the proportion of able seamen to ordinary ... by Sir Anthony Deane...   14

workmen employed in the several yards, 1675   45

list of the seamen ... in every province of France, 1677   46

establishment of ... men and ... guns, 1677 ...   .3, 31, 66

    ,,   ,,   ,,   ,,   ,,   1684   66

general list of ... persons in employment in the admiralty and ...
    navy ... 1687   ...   .   22, 27

Merchants' fleet, resolution concerning the, 1671   45

Midshipmen extraordinary, establishments for, 1676 and 1686   ...   65, 29

Milford Haven, an ancient Discourse and Description of 2, 42

Minutes, Naval   27

Minutes of the commission of the admiralty, 1674–9   26

Miscellaneous Naval Manuscripts [Jac. I]   68

Miscellany of Matters Historical, Political, and Naval   38–63

Moneys, order concerning the transportation of, in the King's ships, 1673...   35

Monson, Sir William :

    propositions for the regulating divers evils in the navy, 1636   52

    Six books of Discourses touching the Navy   25

Morocco, Emperor of 40, 41

Mountgomery's *Book of the Navy* ... 1570 and 1588   5

Moxon [Joseph], tract by   16

Munden, Sir Richard :

    his journal ... relating to his retaking St. Helena ... 1673   15

Muster-master in the narrow seas, instructions to the, 1683 ...   ...   33 (p. 274)

Narbrough, Sir John :

    his journals, 1672–3   ...   .17(2), 39

    appointed a commissioner of the navy, 1686   ...   .28(2), 29

Naval :

    action, account of ... 1654–75   11

    extracts out of ... historians 16, 21

    matters, correspondence in relation to, 1680   45

    papers ... with a report of Mr. Pepys's, 1669   21

    philosophy, Sir William Petty's scheme of   41

    preparations, papers relating to, 1557–8   51

       ,,   making in Holland, 1688   63

Naval Minutes   27

Navigation :

    A Catalogue to Mr. Pepys's books on   21

Navigation—*continued.*   PAGE

Conjectura Nautica, seu Disquisitio de origine Navigationis 6

Bibliotheca Nautica, 1695 20

report concerning trade and ... 1661 42

papers ... touching our yet imperfect attainments in ... 1640, 1696 ... 9

Mr. Flamsteed's account of ... 1697 8

a paper ... concerning 52

Navy and Admiralty Precedents 27

Navy, Discourses of the ... ... 9, 20, 25(2), 42, 43

Navy, scheme for the distribution of the, 1570 6

Navy, state of the :

   articles to be enquired into by the commissioners for the survey of

   the ... 1626? 52

   report on the ... 1642 12

   representations ... of the ill state of ... 1659–60 12

   report of the officers of the navy upon ... 1662 12

   account of the condition of his Majesty's affairs of the navy ... 1673–4 13

   Sir Anthony Deane's observations relating to the ... 1674 45

   Mr. Pepys's general report of the ... 1675 45

   an answer ... by Sir John Tippetts ... 1677 13

   a note of the services done for the advancement of the navy since ...,

   1679 51

   state of the ... navy ... 1684 4

   Mr. Pepys's ... general report of the ill state of the navy ... 1686 ... 67

Navy affairs, an extract of papers ... relating to 27

Navy White Book 18

Norreys, Thomas, his letter to Sir Robert Cotton ... 1608 60

North-east Passage 16

Northampton, Henry Howard, Earl of :

   dedication to, 1604 6

   letters to ... ... 60(3)

Nottingham, Earl of :

   project for contracting the charge of his Majesty's navy 21

   See also "Effingham, Lord Howard of."

Nova Anglorum per mare Cronium ad Moscovitas Navigatio 5

Officers :

   of the crown ... with their fees, *c.* 1587–91 41

   land-officers 31

   of the navy—

      their fees or wages ... [Eliz.] 61

      to lie ... on board of her Majesty's ships ... 1585 51

      the ... duty of the officers ... set down by Sir Robert Cotton ... 54

      the names and duties of ... the then officers 54

Officers—*continued.*   PAGE
    the navy officers' defence...   ...   .   50 (pp. 361, 385)
    additional...instructions for the...treasurer of the navy...1671   36
  of the ordnance—
    fees of [Eliz.]   61
    lists of, 1687   24
  sea-commission officers—
    register of...1660–88   69
    officers allowed...to a ship of each rate...1684   67
  of the yard—
    number of clerks and servants allowed to...   36
  officers wounded at sea—
    establishments for, 1673, 1674   ...   .31(3), 48, 65(2)
Offices :
    general heads of things in the office of...papers and records...to 1621   43
    general state of the office of the lord high admiral...1628–88   ...   62
    order...exempting...officers serving in the navy and yards from
      bearing...office in...parishes, 1663   35
    declaration about the future management of...three great offices...
      1687   61
    antiquity of the office of clerk of the navy...1687   61
Olerone, the Boke of the Lawe of **2, 44**
Orange, Prince of **56, 62**
Orders for...ships...in fashion of war **2**
Ordinary, the general reduction of the...1685   67
Ordnance :
    papers relating to the affairs of the   58
    fees of the officers of the...[Eliz.]   61
    project to keep a registry of...1634   52
    report from the officers of the ordnance shewing the...expense...of
      their office...1660–75   12
    committees...to inspect the...accounts of the...ordnance, 1666   ...   14(3)
    letter to the master of the ordnance accompanying an establishment of
      guns...1677   31
    order...directing what style shall be used...in...letters to the
      master of the ordnance...1679   32
    Rules, Orders, and Instructions for...the Office of the Ordnance, 1683   24
    order...for the march of the train of artillery...   62
See also " Guns."

Palmer, Sir Henry, comptroller of the navy **53, 54**
Parliament :
    a petition...to, touching the haven at Dover, *c.* 1600   40
    Abstract of Naval Papers collected for the Parliament   11

Parliament—*continued.*   PAGE

 addresses from, against the growth of France ... ... 13 (p. 115)
 order for Mr. Pepys's general report of the state of the navy ... 1675 ... 45
 notes for discourse in ... 1675 13
 Mr. Pepys's heads for discourse in ... 1676 41
 references to 19, 20, 44
 See also " Commons, House of."

Parliament Rolls, Index of Matters ... Naval contained in ... the 25
Parochial office, exemption from 35
Passes, papers relating to, 1683 33
Pay :
 the rates of wages in peace and war ... [Edw. III] 2
 fees or wages belonging to the lord high admiral and officers of the
  navy and ordnance ... [Eliz.] 61
 a note shewing the advantage ... from the increase of seamen's wages
  ... 1585 51
 the rates of wages of all officers in every ... ship ... 1587 53
 abuses in connexion with sea-pay [Jac. I] ... ... 59 (p. 263), 60 (p. 427)
 a letter ... concerning the settled allowances given to ... officers ... 1622 43
 a note of the ancient salary of the ... officers of the navy ... 1634 ... 52
 a list of the yearly salaries of officers ... 1660 47
 order ... establishing allowances to vice- and rear-admirals ... 1666,
  1674 ... ... 31, 65 (p. 21); 32, 65 (p. 27)
 order ... establishing pensions to flag-officers ... out of employment,
  1668 ... ... 35, 65 (p. 22)
 salary of the treasurer of the navy, 1673, 1674, 1681 ... ... 62 (p. 269)
 order ... establishing ... half-pay to captains ... 1674 30, 32 (p. 259), 65 (p. 25)
  ,, ,, ,, commanders of squadrons, 1675
             30 (p. 165), 65 (p. 28)
  ,, ,, ,, masters of 1st and 2nd-rate ships,
  1675 ... ... 30, 32, 65
 a table of ... officers ... with their ... wages, 1684 67
 list of ... wages and salaries [in King James II.'s Pocket Book] 1
 establishment ... of rewards for ... land forces, 1685 50
 a table of monthly wages allowed to ... officers and seamen ... 1686 ... 30
  ,, ,, ,, proposed ... to be established ... 1686 ... 31
 salary of the commissioners of the navy, 1686 ... ... 28 (p. 80)
 table for the calculation of wages 31
 ,, of rates of sea-wages per mensem 63
 charges extraordinary relating to ... wages which attend a war 14
Pearse, James, Esq., chyrurgeon-general of the navy :
 instructions to, 1673 36
 warrant of appointment, 1686 32

Pearce, James, Esq.—*continued.*   PAGE

provision...made for...sick and wounded seamen by...1687 ... 62
his account of the manner of appointing chyrurgeons...1688 ... 38

Penn, Sir William :

appointed a commissioner of the navy, 1660 34
his *Naval Collections* 19

Pepys, Samuel, Esq., secretary of the admiralty :

Address to the Duke of York...1668... 11
report touching the...economy of the navy...1669 22
Defence...of the Conduct of the Navy...during the late War...
1669–70 ... ...17, 50 (p. 509)
the navy officers' defence ... ... 50 (pp. 361, 385)
Abstract of Naval Papers collected for the Parliament 11
papers presented to the House of Commons...1675 45
notes for discourse in Parliament...1675 13
Mr. Pepys's heads for discourse in Parliament...1676 41
correspondence with Mr. Evelyn upon naval matters, 1680 45
Mr. Pepys's inquiries to Mr. Shere about shipbuilding...1680 ... 46
patent of appointment as secretary of the admiralty, 1684 ... ... 27, 64
*The State of the...Navy...at the Dissolution of the late Commission
of the Admiralty*...1684 4
My Diary relating to the Commission...for the Recovery of the Navy
...1686 4
Mr. Pepys's proposition upon...the ill state of the navy...1686 ... 67
papers relating to Mr. Pepys's retirement from office, 1689 ... ... 63(4)
his observation upon...the funeral-proceeding for the Queen...1695 58
dedications to 6, 64, 68
letters to ... ... 2, 4, 6, 7, 55, 56(2)
interest in science vi
projected History of the Navy ... ... i, iii
references to 4, 6, 21, 41, 55, 56, 57, 58, 61, 62, 64, 67, 70

Pett, Phineas, Esq., commissioner of the navy :

a large and particular complaint against....c. 1603 59
a journal of...1570–1638 39

Petty, Sir William :

arithmetical observations... 47
essay in political arithmetic... 48
scheme of naval philosophy... 41
papers relating to experiments about shipping, 1683–4 ... 41, 48 (p. 1), 69
letter...touching a travelling chariot, 1685 48

Pilots :

a proposal...for the examining...of pilots [Eliz.] 54
a table of rates...for the piloting of his Majesty's ships... ... 36
instructions to be observed by all...pilots...attending the fleet, 1672 45

Plantations :   PAGE
    a scheme of a history of the... 1680   39
    considerations...concerning...our...plantations in America, 1685   47
Plate-carriage, establishment for, 1686   ...   .   32, 67
Popham, Edward, admiral   61
Ports, a note of all the   53
Portsmouth :
    commissioner at, 1686   ...   .   28, 29
    fleet to be transported to, 1558   2
    harbour at   32
Portugal :
    a note of all the havens in...   47
    the present state of... 1672–3   64
Precedents, Navy and Admiralty   27
Prisoners of war :
    commissioners appointed... for the ordering of... 1672 ...   ...   36 (p. 536)
    instructions to a provost-marshal for taking care of... 1672 ...   36 (p. 548)
Private yard, reasons...why the master-shipwright should not keep a...
    1652   52
Privateer, a commission for a... 1672   48
Prizes :
    the ancient custom...concerning...shares...of...[Eliz.]   30
    a patent for constituting...commissioners for... 1665   37
    rules... to be observed... in the adjudication of... 1665   37
    a collection of papers relating to...   44
Process against Thomas Daniel... 1687   30
Pursers, about taking security from... 1662   34

Queenborough, Inquisition at, 1375   42

Raines, Sir Richard :
    appointed judge of the admiralty, 1686   32
    his opinion upon... two great points... 1688?   38
Rainsford, Richard :
    his project for the prohibiting strangers to fish... 1604   39
Rawlinson MSS., relation of the Pepysian MSS. to the   viii
Registry of seamen, ships, ordnance, etc., 1634   52
Relations of the battle with the Dutch, 28 May, 1672, by the Duke of
    York and others   45
Reprisal 37, 39
Rider, Mr., the case of, stated in arithmetic   47
Rotherhithe (Redrith), Corporation of Shipwrights of   52

Royal Society :   PAGE
   original book of accounts ... in the Library of the ...   .   51 (p. 1)
   a discourse before ... 1675   41
Rupert, Prince :
   proceedings at Kinsale, 1649   38
   appointed vice-admiral of England, 1672   29
     ,,   a commissioner of the admiralty, 1673 ...   .   29, 40, 66
   his commission determined, 1679   ...   .   40 (p. 409)
Russell, Admiral :
   a criticism of his expedition to the Mediterranean ... 1694   15

St. Helena, the retaking of, 1673 ...   .   15, 17
Sallee :
   a list of the ships belonging to ... 1685   50
   the present war with ... 1686   ...   .   34 (p. 344)
Salutes :
   papers relating to   55
   an account of divers things ... about firing and salutes   44
   the ordinance of King John at Hastings about   42
   a paper relating to ... 1670   46
   an abstract of the rules about ... 1685   67
Sandwich, Earl of :
   errors in navigation by ... 1659   9
   appointed vice-admiral of the navy and admiral of the narrow seas,
     1660   29
   appointed admiral in the narrow seas, 1661 ...   .   42(2)
     ,,   ,,   for the then expedition, 1661   42
Scott, Colonel John :
   his history and description of the river of the Amazones   47
   his preface to an intended history of America   47
Sea-Charts, A Set of   70
Sea-Dominion :
   a discourse concerning   58
   a transcript of arguments asserting   39
   an account of divers things concerning   44
   arguments proving the King's exclusive propriety of   59
   Sir Philip Meadows's observations touching   54
Sea-lands :
   arguments proving the King's Majesty's propriety in   39
Sea-manuscripts, classification of Pepysian   i
Search, papers relating to the right of   ...   .   61 (p. 33)
Secretary of the admiralty :
   patent of appointment, 1684   ...   .   27, 64

Sheerness :   PAGE
    commissioner at, 1686   ...   .   28, 29
Shere (or Sheeres), Henry :
    A Discourse touching the Current in the Strait of Gibraltar   4
    Mr. Pepys's enquiries to ... about shipbuilding, 1680   46
Shipbuilding :
    a paper arguing for building ships ... by contract as anno 1589 ...   58
    memoranda of warrants for building and repairing ships ... 1588–90   1
    a view of ... timber-trees ... fit for the repair of her Majesty's ships
    ... 1593   51
    a proportion for ... rigging ... 1611   68
    reasons why the King's ships should be graved ... 1627   52
    certificates ... concerning the worm at Portsmouth, 1630   52
    observations touching contract-ships ... 1652–68   12
    the number of merchant docks in the ... Thames ... 1666   43
    number of shipwrights ... employed ... 1666 and 1667   12
    contract ... about repairing ... 1670   12
    Sir Anthony Deane's *Doctrine of Naval Architecture,* 1670   67
    the state of the Forest of Dean ... 1671   12
    papers relating to the proposal for building 20 new ships, 1674–5   ...   13
    the charge of building ... in his Majesty's yards compared with ...
    contract ... 1675   12
    a particular of ... docks ... as also a list of ... master-shipwrights
    ... 1675 ?   12
    Mr. Tippetts and Commissioner Deane their report about ... ship-
    wrights ... 1675   13
    Commissioner Deane's observations upon ... frigates ... 1675   46
    notes ... about our want and building of ships ... 1676   13
    correspondence about galley-frigates, 1676 ...   .   46 (p. 243)
    the number of shipwrights in England ... 1677   13
    papers relating to the proposed fleet of 90 ships, 1678   13
    ships built by the French since ... 1678   14
    papers relating to the building of 30 new ships, 1679   13
    Mr. Dummer to Mr. Pepys about improving the Art of Building
    Ships, 1679   2
    notes ... concerning the present state of Algiers as to their skill in
    building of ships ... 1680   46
    Mr. Pepys's enquiries to Mr. Shere about shipbuilding ... 1680   ...   46
    Edward Battine's *Method of Building ... Ships of War,* 1684   1
    papers relating to Sir William Petty's ... sluice-bottomed vessel, 1684   48
    a solemn conference ... touching ... east country plank ... 1686   ...   31, 61
    a paper ... concerning ... building of ships, etc.   52
    Collection of Vessels Naval   68
    Fragments of Ancient English Shipwrightry   23

Shipbuilding—*continued.*   PAGE
  Mr. Deane's Method of Measuring ... a Ship......   16
  Of Navarchi   5
Shipping :
  a remonstrance ... from Trinity House of the decay of ... 1602   ... 39
  reasons touching the maintenance of ... 1609   39
  papers relating to Sir William Petty's experiments about ... 1683–4 ... 41
Ships, abstracts, accounts, and lists of :
  Anthony Anthony's *Declaration of the Royal Navy of England ...*
    1546   70
  Anthony Anthony's *Declaration of the Royal Navy of England ...*
    1546 (Abstract)   10
  a list of ships ... 1557   ... ... 51 (p. 10)
  a declaration ... of the Queen's and hired ships ... 1559 2
  a certificate of ... shipping in the Cinque Ports ... 1563 and 30 years
    before   51
  a list of ships built ... 1571–6 51
  an abstract of a certificate ... of ... ships ... belonging to the Five
    Ports ... 1587   53
  the number of ships ... returned in the year 1588 53
  the number ... of the ships retained in the wars of ... Edward III ... 2
  a note ... of all the shipping in the havens of Spain and Portugal   47 (p. 503)
  a list of the Low Country ships ... 1588   51
  an abstract of the ... fleet set forth ... against the Spanish Armada...
    1588   53
  a list of all the ships ... of her Majesty's fleet ... 1590 54
  a certificate of ships ... in the ports ... of Essex, Suffolk, Norfolk,
    Kent, and Sussex ... 1591   54
  a list of ships built ... since 33 Eliz. ... 1597   54
  an abstract ... of every ship ... 1600–77   11
  a list of the King's ships ... 1604   40
  a catalogue of all the King's ships ... 1607 ...   . 40, 47
  a list of ships [Jac. I]   68
  A Book of all the shipping ... within the vice-admiralty of ... South
    ... *Devon,* 1619 7
  the royal navy of England ... 1633   46
  a list of the King's ships ... 1642   12
  a list of the new frigates built by the Parliament ... 1646–53 47
  a list of all ships ... belonging to the State's navy ... 1652   47
  merchant-ships hired to serve as men-of-war ... 1652–3, 1665–7 12
  abstract of ... the two fleets of ... 1660 and 1676 compared   11
  the naval force of England ... 1660 and ... 1678 compared 14
  a letter concerning a list of merchant-ships ... fit for his Majesty's
    service ... 1665   43

Ships, abstracts, accounts, and lists of—*continued.*   PAGE

    A *List of His Majesty's Fleet ... employed against Holland,* 1671, 1672,
        and 1673   1

    ships built by the King of France since ... 1672   13

    the present fleets of English, French, and Dutch, 1673   13

    a list of the French fleet as ... taken in ... 1673   46

    a list of the fleet of the United Provinces as ... taken in ... 1673   46

    a list of the French fleet abroad ... 1673   46

    an abstract of the number of men-of-war ... etc., employed in the last
        war in 1673   13

    a list of French ships and galleys, 1674   12

    a list of the English, French, and Dutch fleets, 1675   ...   ...   12 (No. 13)

    an abstract of the ... numbers and force of the present fleets of Eng-
        land, France, and Holland 12, 13, 14, 46

    instances of the great burdens and force of ships of the French and
        Dutch   12

    ships repaired ... in the several yards ... 1675   45

    a list of his Majesty's fleet ... 1675   45

    a list of all his Majesty's ships ... [1675]   45

    monthly lists of the ships at sea ... 1675   45

    a list of the French fleet, 1676   13

    the navy of France ... 1677   46

    an account of the galleys of France ... 1677   46

    a general list of the royal navy ... 1684   64

    an account of the disposal of ... ships ... in sea-pay ... 1684   67

    a list of the ... ships in the port of Brest ... 1684   47

    an account of the ... corsairs of Algiers ... 1685   53

    a list of his Majesty's ships ... 1685   62

    the general list of the French fleet ... 1685   50

    a list of all men-of-war belonging to Algiers, 1685 ...   .   50 (p. 267)

    a list of the ships belonging to Sallee ... 1685   50

    the naval force of Tunis, 1685 ...   .   50 (p. 233)

    list of ships in *King James II's Pocket Book*   1

    the present state of the shipping of Amsterdam ... 1686   62

    a general list of the ships of the royal navy, 1687   27

    the present disposal of ... ships in sea-pay, 1687   31

    an account of the present force of Algiers by sea, 1687   ...   . 31, 61

    the naval force of ... Sweden ... 1688   61

    a collection of papers containing the number, names, etc. ... of every
        ship ... of the royal navy of England ... 1688   63

    the naval forces of the Czar of Muscovy, 1699   63

    A *Register of the Ships of the Royal Navy of England* ... 1660–88   ...   69

Ships, names of :

	PAGE			PAGE			PAGE
Advantage	61	Falcon	33	Leopard	23
Anne	19	Florence (Spanish)	44	Margaret galley	61
Anne	37	Formosa	18	Mary yacht	56
Assistance	17	Four Brothers	37	Mordaunt	33
Bear galleon	8	Francis...	50	Murrian	71
Castle frigate fire-ship	15	Hampton Court	3	Phœnix	33
		Harry Grace à Dieu	71	Prince	17, 39
Charles galley	5	Henrietta	20	Prosperous pink	16
Charlotte yacht	56	Henry	43	Return	47
Crown	12	Jersey	20	St. Michael	17
Dover	12	Jerusalem	30	Saudades	63
Dragon	34	Judith	8	Speedwell	16
Fairfax	17	Leicester	8	Struse	71
		Lennox	3		

See also p. 68, where the names of thirty ships surveyed in 1611 are given.

Shipwrights, Company of :
    a bill for ... timber, prepared ... with the joint care of the Company of ... 1675 ... 41
    an account of ... the proceedings had ... between the Brotherhood ... and the new Corporation of ... 1683-4 ... 52
    papers relating to the Shipwrights' Company, 1684-5 ... 50

Shish, Mr. John ... 3(2)

Sick and wounded seamen :
    commissioners appointed ... for ... 1672 ... 36(5)
    a collection of papers containing ... establishments for ... 1672 ... 48
    moneys paid for ... 1672, 1673 ... 14
    the establishment about cripples ... 1674 ... 67
    a collection of papers containing ... the standing rules of relief to mariners ... maimed ... 1685 ... 48
    the provision ... made for .. 1687 ... 62
    the disposal of ... 1688 ... 38 (p. 628)
See also "Officers."

Slyngesbie, Sir Robert :
    his *Discourse of the Navy*, 1660 ... 9, 43

Southwell, Sir Robert :
    his discourse before the Royal Society ... touching water, 1675 ... 41

Southwold Bay, the battle of ... 9, 45 (p. 137)

Spain :
    a note of the musters of persons of all qualities in, 1588 .. 47
    a project for the sea in opposition to ... [Eliz.] ... 52
    a note of all the havens in ... 47

Spain—*continued.* PAGE

   the opinion of ... sea-captains whether it be best for the fleet ... to lie
on our coast ... or to go to the coast of Spain ... 1626   52

Spanish Armada 14, 22, 53

Storekeepers' accounts, Mr. Hosier's method of balancing, 1668   6

Stores :

   abuses about ... [Jac. I] ...   .   60 (pp. 380, 427)

   report ... touching ... stores ... 1662 ...   .   12 (No. 15)

   a copy of the report from the committees appointed to inspect the
accounts of the ... stores ... 1666   ...   .   14 (No. 152)

   an abstract of the prices given ... for ... stores ... 1668–75   12

   advice ... touching an establishment for boatswains' and carpenters'
sea-stores ... 1686   38

Strickland, Sir Roger :

   his designs of distinction for vice- and rear-admirals   57

   letters about flags, 1686–7   ...   .   56(3)

Strode, Colonel, governor of Dover Castle   6

Sunderland, Lord   30

Superannuation :

   order ... establishing allowances to superannuated officers ... 1672   ...   31, 66

   form of warrant for ... a pension   32

Surveys of ships 2, 52, 68

Tangier :

   correspondence ... concerning Tangier ... 1683   ...   .40(2), 41

   references to 33, 34, 64

Thames (or "the River") :

   the number of ... wherrymen on the ... 1583   54

   a device how to secure ... against ... foreign galleys ... 1600   53

   a letter concerning a list of merchant ships ... in the ... 1665   43

   the number of merchant docks in the ... 1666   43

   papers relating to the conservancy of the ... mainly 1684–5   62

   A State of the Shores on each side of the Thames ... 1684 *and* 1687 ...   71

   form of ... licence to a waterman or wherryman to row in the   38

Thomas, William, clerk to the privy council :

   his letter to King Edward VI   40

Tickets   52

Tippetts, Sir John :

   his report about shipwrights, 1675   ...   .   13 (p. 62)

   his answer to Mr. Pepys about naval force, 1677 ...   .   13 (p. 115)

   appointed a commissioner of the navy, 1686   ...   .28(2), 29

Tobermory ("Tippermory"), Spanish wreck at ...   .   44(2)

Tower, the :   PAGE
   the names of all the prisoners in ... 1549   40
   records of   6
Trade :
   report ... concerning ... trade ... 1661   42
   lists of English merchants trading in Portugal, 1672–3   64
   several considerations relating to ... 1684   47
Trevor, Sir John, surveyor of the navy :
   instructions ... for the ordering of receipts and issues of provisions
   ... 1603   68
   references to ... ...   54, 60(2)
Trevor, Sir John :
   lends manuscripts to Pepys 10, 24
Trevor Papers, Transcript of the Index to the   24
Trevoriana, Collectiones   10
Trinity House, the :
   King Henry VIII's ... charter to   38
   Queen Elizabeth's charter to   38
   a collection of papers relating to the affairs of ... 1513–1687   62
   the opinion of ... touching shares in time of war ... 1594   39
   a petition from ... touching the haven at Dover, c. 1600   40
   a remonstrance ... from ... of the decay of shipping and mariners
   ... 1602   39
   a petition from ... touching the maintenance of English shipping
   ... 1609   39
   a letter concerning a list of merchant-ships ... from ... 1665   43
   copies of three addresses from ... 1681, 1682, and 1683   62
   surveys of the Thames, by ... 1684 and 1687   71
   a table of rates adjusted by ... for piloting   36
   reference to   9
   forms of certificates and licences from ... ...   38(3)
Tunis, naval force of, 1685 ... ...   50 (p. 233)

Ubaldino, Petruccio, *A Discourse concerning the Spanish Fleet* ... 1688 ...   22
Union of English and French fleets, agreement for the, 1672   46 (pp. 219, 231, 233)

Vario (Verrio), Signor, the King's painter   58
Vice-Admirals :
   the duties of the ... and their sub-officers   30
Victualling :
   an indenture ... relating to ... victualling ... 1564   53
   papers relating to the victualling of the navy, 1590   54

Victualling—*continuea.*   PAGE
instructions ... for the ordering of receipts and issues of provisions
    ... 1603   68
abuses of   59–60
articles towards the amendment of the victualler's contract ... 1612 ...   54
extract of the several contracts ... from 1612 to 1660 ... with an
    abstract of ... accounts ... 1625–42   48
copy of his Majesty's contract ... 1623   52
order ... to survey ... the same, 1626   52
observations on the management of the surveyor-general of ... *c.* 1665   43
a calculation of the profit arising upon   43
memorandum relating to victuals at Livorne, 1667   18
a project for commanders having the charge ... of ... with a discourse
    touching victualling by contract, 1673   43
remarks ... by Lord Dartmouth ... upon the foregoing project   43
an abstract of the victualling declarations ... 1673–86   67
contract ... for ... the Mediterranean ... 1674   35
a table of "broken proportions"   35
provisions in the victualling stores ... 1675   45
the contract for ... 1677   35
a supplemental contract ... for ... the Mediterranean, 1677   35
patent constituting ... commissioners for ... 1683   28
Vincent, Nathaniel, *Conjectura Nautica*   6
Virginia ... Journals relating to, 1676–7   18
Volunteers :
order ... establishing rewards to ... 1673   ...   ...   31 (p. 219), 67 (p. 83)
his Majesty's establishment of the number, qualifications, and duties
    of ... 1676   65
an establishment about ... 1686   29
Voyages and Journals :
A Collection of Sea Journals ... 1684   16
Bolland's *Mediterranean Journal,* 1676   64
Chancelor, Richard, to Muscovy, 1553   5
Cox, John, into the South Seas, 1680–2   15
Cowley, William Ambrosia, round the globe, 1683–6   24
East India Company's ship "Return" upon the Coast of Japan, 1673   47
Fenton, Edward, to Meta Incognita, 1578, and towards China, 1582–3   8
Holmes, Captain Robert, into Guinea, 1660–1 and 1663–5   20
Jenifer, Captain James, to Lisbon, 1672–3   63
Munden, Sir Richard, to St. Helena, 1673 ...   .   15, 17
Narbrough, Captain John, on board the Prince, 1672 ...   .   17, 39
    ,,   ,,   ,,   ,,   Fairfax, 1672–3   17
    ,,   ,,   ,,   ,,   St. Michael, 1673   17

Voyages and Journals—*continued*.   PAGE
    Poole, Benjamin, to Newfoundland, 1677–8   23
    Sharpe, Captain Bartholomew, in the South Seas, 1680–2   ...   ...19, 50(2)
    Waters, Benjamin, towards Bantam, 1677–8   18
    Willshaw, Thomas, to St. Helena, 1673   15
    Wood, Captain John, for the discovery of the N.E. Passage, 1676 ...   16

Warrant, forms of   ...   .   32(2)
Wells, Mr., his proposal about cordage   18
White, Sir Richard :
    considerations ... concerning Jamaica, etc. ... 1685   47
Widows and orphans :
    order ... appointing ... commissioners for ... widows and orphans ...
    1673   ...   .33 (p. 335), 48 (p. 47), 66 (p. 67)
    an abstract of ... instructions ... for the relief of widows, etc. ...
    1673?   ...   .   36 (p. 551)
    order to the navy board ... 1674 (with subsequent extensions) ...   34 (p. 342)
    order ... for allowing relief to ... 1688   ...   .   35 (p. 481)
Wiggs, Thomas :
    letters ... complaining of ... Sir John Hawkyns ... 1588   ...   ...   60, 61
    discoveries concerning abuses ... 1599   60
Williamson, Sir Joseph 22, 61
Woolwich :
    commissioner at, 1686   ...   .   28, 29
Worm, the   52
Wounded, *see* "Officers," and "Sick and wounded seamen."
Wynter, William, Esq. :
    admiral's instructions made by ... 1558   2

Yarmouth, herring fishery at   ...   .   33 (p. 313)
York, James, Duke of ("his Royal Highness") :
    a commission ... constituting him lord high admiral ... 1661 ...   ...   40, 66
    his commission to the Earl of Sandwich ... 1661 ...   .   42 (p. 599)
    his letter to the navy board directing their ... reforming ... abuses
    ... 1662   34
    warrant ... [and] ... book of ... general instructions ... 1662   34
    his letter ... about ... taking security from ... pursers ... 1662   34
    S.P.'s Address to the Duke ... 1668, with ... proceedings upon the same   11
    his letter to the commissioners of the navy reflecting upon [them] ...
    1668   35
    his letter ... upon their answer to his letter of reflections ... 1668   ...   35

York, James, Duke of (" his Royal Highness ")—*continued.*   PAGE

   Mr. Pepys's report touching the ... economy of the navy ... presented
     from the navy board to ... the Duke ... 1669   22

   his order allowing the commissioners of the outports to act ... 1670 ...   34

   his letter to the navy board accompanying ... additional ... instruc-
     tions for the ... treasurer of the navy ... 1671   36

   the French King's commission to the Duke ... to be commander-in-
     chief ... 1672   46

   the Duke of York's sailing instructions, 1672   45

    ,,   ,,   fighting instructions, 1672   45

   relations of the battle with the Dutch, 28th May, 1672, by the Duke
     [and others]   45

   petition to, 1683   ...   .   44 (p. 510)

   references to   ...   .   X, 2, 20, 34, 39, 43, 46, (p. 233), 55

Lightning Source UK Ltd.
Milton Keynes UK
UKHW010619040419
340475UK00001B/31/P